WRITING
FOR A LIVING

WRITING
FOR A LIVING

IAN LINTON

SECOND EDITION

Kogan Page
WORKING
for
YOURSELF
Series

First published in Great Britain in 1985
by Kogan Page Limited
120 Pentonville Road
London N1 9JN

Reprinted 1985
Second edition 1988

British Library Cataloguing in Publication Data

Linton, Ian
    Writing for a living. — 2nd ed. — (Kogan Page
    working for yourself series).
    1. Authorship — Vocational guidance —
    Great Britain
    I. Title
    808'.02'02341   PN153

    ISBN 1-85091-461-3

Printed in Great Britain by
Biddles Ltd, Guildford

Contents

Introduction

A writer, according to the novelist John Braine, is someone who counts words. That statement destroys much of the myth and romance surrounding the life of the professional writer. Anyone who wishes to write for a living must realise that his or her income comes from producing a specified number of words by a given date.

When one piece of writing is complete the process begins again. The number of words you produce earn different rates of pay — £100 for a 2000-word article, £500 advance for a book of 50,000 words, £4000 in royalties for a book over a period of time. These are just random examples, and rates vary enormously. None of those figures comes anywhere near the magic figure known as average income. Perhaps you don't need that level of income, perhaps you are a person of independent means, but most people have a family to support and need the money. Writing is an occupation where you cannot expect to earn a regular income without careful planning. On the other hand, the life of a writer is largely self-created and so are the rewards. No one forces you to write a particular book or play. There are no 9 to 5 working hours, though you need to impose discipline on yourself, and the deadlines are largely of your own choosing. This is not a recipe for a lax life. The disciplines of professional pride, interest in your work, and the need to earn a living counteract any other tendencies.

Who needs writers?

This book is about the opportunities that are open to a writer. Who needs writers, why they need them, and what they are looking for. What might begin as a short list of opportunities soon grows considerably. Magazine articles, books, radio talks, company brochures, newspaper columns, film scripts, television, plays, educational work, editorial services — the list continues. What the professional writer needs to know is that there are enough interesting and money-earning opportunities to commit a life to writing.

The basis of writing income

In the sections on sales opportunities in different media and on finance, the various forms of income are discussed. Broadly speaking these fall into two main categories — fees and royalty payments.

Fees are paid for a service, writing the text for a company report, for example, or for the right to reproduce an author's work once only, a television play, or a magazine article; sometimes for books. The fee does not vary with the size of the audience, although it may vary between publications or television programmes. So an article in the *Daily Mirror* might earn more than an article in the *Colchester Evening Gazette*, but if a promotion helped to boost *Daily Mail* sales by a few thousand, the author would still receive the same fee.

Payment for books, however, is usually related to the number of copies sold. The author is paid a royalty on each copy sold and there are also a number of subsidiary rights whose proceeds are paid directly to the author, or may be shared between author and publisher.

Whatever form of payment you receive you should retain the copyright in your work. The laws of copyright are complex but basically they protect the work you have created from improper copying by someone else. When a publisher pays you royalties he is paying for the right to reproduce your work in the form of a book and you receive payment for each copy that is sold. A magazine or television and radio company pays you a fee for the right to reproduce your work in a specified form on one single occasion only. Beyond this simple distinction the subject of fees becomes more complicated and is covered in the appropriate section.

It's not where you've been

The full-time writer does not appear by magic or wake up one morning and declare him or herself a writer. Normally you would have served some kind of apprenticeship, either writing as part of another occupation or having some published success from part-time writing. That initial success is likely to encourage you into thinking that, given time, you could be more successful. Writing is a time-consuming business, and it can be difficult to achieve your aims in the confines of evenings or weekends. It can be done, but it can also be frustrating.

There are some occupations where you do a lot of writing — working as a reporter, in a publicity department, an advertising agency, public relations consultancy, or an editorial consultancy. The limitation is that the material you write is not your own choosing. It is, however, practising the mechanics of writing, usually against a deadline, and that in itself is a good discipline. An academic career can also involve a considerable amount of writing on subjects which would certainly be of your choosing.

It's where you're going to

This level of writing may be sufficient for some people, but others want to spend all their time writing. If you are fortunate enough you can be forced into becoming a full-time writer; you may have had some initial published success and you have now been commissioned to carry out more extensive work. Full-time writing has become a practical necessity.

It is important to establish that the opportunities for writing on the topics you know will continually be available. Magazines can close, other experts can move in, editors change and eventually the opportunities disappear. You need to know that you can change direction if necessary. That doesn't mean you need encyclopaedic knowledge, but it does mean that you should be able to transfer writing ability to other subjects.

Your initial investment

When a writer does decide to go ahead, there is little investment needed to establish a business. The equipment needed is minimal — a typewriter and a writing surface. Basic running costs are also low — postage, stationery and the cost of photography (if you plan to illustrate your material). The business can get more complicated but the ratio of expense to income is never very high.

The main investment is that of time, not just time spent writing, but for research, correspondence, consultation with publishers and planning future work. The time available must be sufficient to complete projects on time. Where you live is immaterial, although practical matters like travelling to meetings or delivering work can prove a problem. That really depends on the sort of work you want to handle; if the job requires lots of meetings and regular consultation, you need to be close to the business. But if you only produce material which requires minimal consultation, then location is no problem. All you need is a post office.

Building a business

What a professional writer needs is customers to write for, people who will pay for the text. Your customers could include publishers, editors, publicity managers, television producers, training managers — anyone who needs words.

If you have already sold some of your writing you will be aware of the demands of your market and of the material you need to supply. However, the market for writing is very wide and some of the areas may be unfamiliar. You do not know what the customers are looking for, where to send your work, whom to deal with, or how to present your work. You may be unsure of the rewards of that part of the market, or whether you have the skills and knowledge to succeed.

Planning your route

Writing for a Living aims to answer those questions. It is a map, not a guide book. It can tell you where to go, but it does not make the journey for you. You succeed or fail by your own ability. The book assumes that you know how to write and what to write; it tells you how to reach the person who is buying.

Most writers begin with published success in one field but the skills of writing are the same whatever the medium. The selling skills are different though. Chapter 1 shows how to make initial approaches in each of the main markets, and how to find out what the opportunities are.

Individual chapters on each of the main areas of writing cover research, opportunities, proposals, contacts and payments in more detail. They include magazines and newspapers, books — fiction, non-fiction and children's — radio and television, feature films, audio visual, poetry and the theatre, education, business communications, teaching and editorial services.

Whatever areas you decide to concentrate on you need to build up a regular flow of work quickly. Chapter 1 shows you how to use initial success and build on it. By getting a mix of work that is published at frequent intervals you can earn a regular income.

Presenting work

One of the factors that can affect your success is the way you present work. A good manuscript makes life easier for the reader and helps to make your work more acceptable. It is equally important to make the best possible use of photographs and illustrations. Chapter 11 summarises the proper way to prepare manuscripts and the information you need to brief photographers and illustrators. It also stresses the need for accuracy in proof-reading.

Writing is a low investment business, but modern technology in the shape of computers and word processors can help the writer operate more efficiently and cope with text changes easily. Chapter 12 discusses the way in which you can use these aids.

Running the business

Every business needs professional advice at some stage — on finance, legal matters, marketing or running the business. Chapters 13 and 15 outline the services that are available and discuss other people who can contribute to your business — designers, illustrators, printers, photographers and marketing specialists.

Finance is a particularly difficult problem in a writing business. You don't have a product to sell that gives you an immediate cash payment. You have to wait until publication or completion of a project to earn money, and income can be spread over a long period. The time-scale for book royalties is years rather than months. Chapter 13 shows how copy dates, lead times, publication dates and the type of work you handle can all affect the amount and timing of your income. Getting a regular income from writing is a careful balancing act.

If you are successful as an individual writer you may have to expand and employ other writers to cope with the workload. 'Running a Writing Business' discusses the way in which a writing company operates and considers the very different aspects of being an employer. Chapter 14 also looks at some of the successes of individual writers including those who have managed to combine the career of author and publisher.

Chapter 1

Getting Sales and Developing a Workload

There are many opportunities for a writer, but there are also a lot of writers. No one owes anybody a living. A professional writer has to get out and sell: not an easy task, because you are not selling a commodity like a book or magazine. You are selling a service, something that will help the customers improve their business — helping the editor put together a magazine, a publisher produce books, a television producer create a play, or a businessman promote his products.

Research

Before you write for someone else you have to know what that person will produce. Your writing does not have an independent life, it is part of his or her product. Research is important. You have to know what types of book are on a publisher's list, what audience a magazine is aiming at, the programmes a producer is working on, and many other factors. This is the market you write for and you need a good long-term view of where to direct your work.

Basic research is one of the most important stages in setting up a writing business. You have to look beyond the first magazine article, book, television script or company brochure for continuity of work. You want to know that the publisher or producer who buys your work can offer you many other opportunities. The 70/30 ratio is a pattern that applies to many types of business. It states that 70 per cent of a company's sales will come from 30 per cent of its customers. The ratio could be even higher but the implication is that most of a company's work will come from repeat buying. Repeat buying has a much lower risk factor, the buyer knows that you can deliver and that your quality is good.

Translated into writing terms that means it is easier to sell your second article or book to a publisher. The publisher is no longer taking a risk on your abilities. The hardest way to build a business is to be continually approaching new customers.

14

In your research you should look for the long-term opportunities — magazines that publish your type of article every month, series of books that you can extend, companies with a large promotional budget.

The type of research you do depends on the work you are looking for but, if you are writing for publication, the best starting place is the *Writers' and Artists' Year Book*. It lists most of the book, magazine and newspaper publishers in the UK, and in many overseas countries. As far as possible it indicates the sort of manuscripts publishers are looking for. Television and radio companies are listed as well as groups of people offering opportunities or useful services to writers.

The reference sources mentioned throughout this book can help your initial planning, but you need to get into the newsagents and bookshops, watch television and study the theatre and film guides to get a better indication of the scope of a publisher or production company.

Research should be a continuous process. It is essential if you are starting a business, but you need to keep up to date with publishers' policy changes, changes in editorship, success or failure, and the popularity of different topics. It is easy to lose your sense of direction when you are under pressure to meet completion dates.

Contacts

If your research is good you should now have a variety of opportunities. There are no barriers to new writers but much depends on the professionalism of the person you are trying to sell to.

The publisher and editor are looking for good writing but they are first and foremost in the market for a product that they can sell — a proposal or manuscript which will become a book or magazine article. They take the writer's skill on trust and assume that at the end of the day you will produce a good piece of work. These are the professional buyers.

You also meet people who could use writing services, but don't realise they are in the market for them. You are more likely to find them if you are writing business publications. Here there is a two-stage selling operation. That sort of person believes anyone can write. What you as a professional writer need to establish is that you can do it much better. It is sometimes difficult to convince someone who normally does his or her own writing that it can be improved, but that is a problem that anyone marketing professional services faces.

Manuscript or proposal

Since you need to earn money from the work you produce, and not waste time on text that cannot be sold, you should make your first approach with a letter of enquiry. That establishes whether the work you are offering is of interest. A similar book may have been recently published, the editor may have commissioned someone else to write on the subject, or you may have completely misjudged the market. If the response is positive you may have a buyer.

Editors may accept complete articles without a preliminary letter, but you always run the risk of wasted effort. If you are writing a book you need to make that preliminary enquiry and submit a synopsis. A synopsis is a brief outline showing the main topics to be covered in the book. It could be a numbered list of important topics or a list of section/chapter headings with the main topics in each. It shows the publisher that you have a grasp of the subject.

Only 1 to 2 per cent of unsolicited book manuscripts are accepted for publication. Publishers have many factors to consider when they are assessing a book. They have to weigh production and selling costs against probable income. The costs are not inconsiderable — editing, designing, typesetting, paper, printing, binding, distribution and promotion. Income depends on the size of audience for the book. The publisher doesn't need a manuscript to assess that. In television it's the opposite. Only when you are an established writer can you have work commissioned on the basis of a synopsis.

Even after the initial approval there is no guarantee that your work will be finally accepted. The next stage is to provide a detailed manuscript or synopsis. But until you get a contract or firm acceptance there is no sale.

Dealing with rejection

Rejection by one publisher or buyer does not mean the end of the road for your work. You should have a list of alternative markets to try. There is plenty of competition in publishing and broadcasting so you should always persevere. Tales abound of the manuscript that was rejected by the first 20 publishers and then became a bestseller. Unless your work is very specialised there is always one more television station or one more magazine. You may have to modify your material to suit the final buyer but the major part of your work will still be usable. New writers can take heart from George Bernard Shaw's much quoted habit of decorating his bedroom walls with rejection slips.

Commissioned work

The ideal situation is where you are commissioned to produce work to a particular brief. It may be because you have had a previous published or broadcast success in your field and you are now asked to produce more of the same. The commission needn't come from an organisation you are already dealing with. Someone may have seen your work and want you to do something similar for him or her. That cuts down the sales effort you have to make but you need to have a high level of visibility to be noticed by publishers. You need to get among the candidates.

One way is to advertise your special skills in the editorial services section of a publication like *Writers' and Artists' Year Book*. You can use direct mail to contact a select list of publishers and tell them about your experience, areas of knowledge and publication record. This is not the same as a letter offering a specific manuscript. Here you are trying to get yourself on the list of suitable writers when work is being commissioned.

Using an agent

Another way to get sales is to use an agent. If you write fiction or television material you are more likely to need an agent than if you write non-fiction or magazine articles. Many agents would take the same view: the sales and earnings from magazine articles and non-fiction are lower and would give the agent a low return.

Many agents are members of the Association of Authors' Agents and they agree to follow a code of practice which governs their terms of business and the level of services they offer. Their normal charge is 10 per cent of the royalties or fee that you earn for work placed by them in the UK market. If they sell your work overseas they charge a higher percentage because they in turn have to pay another agent abroad.

17

Agents vary in the type of work they handle. In *Writers' and Artists' Year Book* they list the medium — television, film, stage, or books — and the form — synopsis, full manuscript or preliminary letter. Some agents offer a reading service for which they charge a fee. They read and assess your manuscript and give you a report on it. If it is suitable for publication and they place it you may get a refund of the reading fee. If they feel that your manuscript has merit but is not up to publication standard they may suggest revisions and recommend someone to do the work.

Using an agent has a number of advantages. Agents are experienced in selling and, if they take responsibility for that, you can get on with writing. They know the sort of manuscripts that are in demand and in that sense they act as a clearing house between author and publisher. They can assess the merit and potential of a manuscript and they can save wasted effort.

A good agent can negotiate better terms for you. Agents are aware of market rates and they can often improve on the terms in a standard contract. They are also good at selling subsidiary rights for you. Since they are taking 10 per cent of whatever figure they can negotiate, it is in their interests to go for the highest possible sum. They administer royalties and fees for you, and make sure that you receive prompt payment.

Developing a workload

One of the most difficult problems for a full-time writer is developing the right level of work. There are several factors to consider. Where do you want to get to? Are there intermediate stages to go through to secure certain types of work? What are the lead times for the sort of work you are interested in, that is, copy dates, preparation time, and interval between work and payment? More important for the full-time writer, what level of income are you aiming at and will the workload sustain it?

Lead times

Workload must be related to income. You may be commissioned to write several books, but if you have no other income you could have financial problems. Lead times and schedules are the basis for planning. Where the work is commissioned or you are working on a contract basis, schedules are easy to establish. In business writing, for example, companies are working to production and marketing schedules, so any support material has to tie in with these. An advertising budget would be worked out on an annual basis with key dates fixed for most events. The writer would be given a detailed timetable with budget figures. That part of the workload is well established.

If you are writing books you will also be working on predictable lead times. The contract stipulates a completion date and you have to work backwards from that. If you are working exclusively on that project during the time, the only problem is going to be money. There would be an advance from the publisher, which is payable in parts, but that is unlikely to be a large figure unless the book is a potential bestseller. So if the book is likely to occupy a major portion of your time, make sure that you have planned your finances accordingly.

Magazine work becomes predictable only when it is commissioned. Then you have fixed dates for copy, publication and payment, and it enables you to schedule the work. But with normal one-shot magazine work, you are at the mercy of the magazine. You might determine your own writing schedule for producing articles but there is no guarantee of publication date.

Workload

It's important to look at your commitments over a period of a year, or longer if you are able, to see what your workload is. There could be bottlenecks, or very large gaps. There might be total overload, or you might have the opportunity to take on a lot more work. It should become apparent where the gaps are, if any.

If there is a large gap like a month or more when you are between projects you could fit in something like a small book. If you are primarily a magazine writer there may be monthly or weekly gaps where you haven't got an article going into publication. You need to work back from publication dates to see what you might be able to fit in.

An ideal initial spread of work would be a mix of material being published at different time spans. This could include weekly newspaper material, monthly magazine articles, company work every few months, and perhaps one or two books every year. That spreads both the workload and the payments you receive.

Developing work

Now you have published work, you have contacts and you have

material that commands an audience; the problem is how to build on that.

The editor who buys once is likely to buy again provided your work is up to standard and is supplied on time.

Your topic may form the basis of a series or can be used as a regular feature. In a business magazine that could mean a regular electronics feature, for example, where you become the special contributor, and write all the articles on that particular topic.

One way to establish a regular workload is to become a contributing editor, or a special subject editor. American magazines usually employ numbers of regional and special editors. British magazines have special editors, but their numbers are more limited. As a contributing editor you have a greater continuity of work and you also have more say in the way the material is presented.

However, it does limit the number of other magazines that you can write for. As a contributing editor, you are almost a member of staff, and that demands a certain amount of loyalty. As a freelance writer there is nothing to stop you rewriting articles for different publications — a profitable way of making use of previously researched material. You should not repeat material that is already published. Apart from the fact that each market needs a different approach, word soon gets around that material is being recycled. Nor should you send the same material to different publishers simultaneously. However, you could send different versions of an article on crafts to the Sunday supplements, craft magazines, women's magazines, and a regional magazine without overlap.

Book sales

Book sales can expand in the same way. You can write different books on the same subject area for your existing publisher or for different publishers. The terms of a contract between author and publisher stipulate that the writer should not publish any competitive material for a specific period without first offering this to the existing publisher. This is to protect the publisher's investment in the initial book. The publisher is first in the market, and although a successful book will attract a host of imitations, they should not come from the original author.

However, if your new book is not a repeat of the old one, and if the publisher does not wish to take up the option, then you are free to take the book elsewhere. The most satisfying way to build on your knowledge is to write a series on the same subject — a history series, for example, a trilogy of novels, or further titles in a do-it-yourself series. It is building on familiar ground and on published success.

Newspapers

If you are writing primarily for newspapers there is the opportunity to have work published at more frequent intervals than in any other medium. With daily, evening, weekly and Sunday newspapers at national, regional and local levels there is a strong demand for news and feature material.

Few newspapers are directly competitive with each other so you have the opportunity to use similar material in many different publications. An article on a craftswoman, for example, could be used in a Sunday supplement, as a general interest story in the women's page of a national daily, and in the relevant regional and local newspapers as a story of local interest. The article would be rewritten with a different slant each time, but the core would remain the same.

Syndication services, discussed on page 89, are another way of achieving multiple sales of the same article. An agency with contacts in UK and overseas newspapers sells the material you submit to a variety of non-competitive publications, and takes a commission on the sale.

Overseas sales

Overseas sales can be an unexpected source of income if your material is relevant. Much depends on the subject. If you are writing textbooks or instructional articles your material would have to be edited or rewritten to suit the educational, legal or business requirements of the country. Fiction would normally be translated into the language of the country; then it may lose something in translation, or it may be culturally unacceptable in some countries. Overseas sales are not a guaranteed option.

Finding overseas markets is the other part of the problem. English-speaking countries have always been regarded as an extension to the home market for British books and articles with the USA and Commonwealth countries taking the bulk of sales. *Writers' and Artists' Year Book*, and *British Rate and Data* are both good sources of information on overseas media and publishers, while larger local libraries keep catalogues of overseas publications in their reference sections.

Literary agents and syndication agencies usually have contacts in overseas markets, and will try to place the work for you. They charge a commission on the sale which is higher than the UK rate because more administrative work is involved, and they may have to pay another local agent. Book contracts have clauses to cover the author's terms and rights on overseas sales, and publishers will try to sell overseas rights (see page 39).

Writing services for business

Companies buy writing services to support their publicity and training programmes. They do not buy for publication unless they are sponsoring textbooks or films or commissioning a history of the company. Your approach to companies is very different from approaches to publishers. You are offering to carry out writing tasks quickly and to higher standards than the clients could achieve themselves. You need to demonstrate high professional standards showing how you have worked for clients of similar standing, and that you have professional competence in that market area.

Your research efforts should be concentrated on identifying the right contact within a company and finding out about the company and its products. Direct mail is an effective method of contacting business clients but you need to back this with personal presentation, showing examples of your previous work and discussing the client's requirements. Some clients want to take on the combined skills of writer and designer, working as a team, so it could pay to cooperate. You can also work for business clients indirectly by writing for service companies that supply them — advertising agencies, public relations consultancies, design groups or printers. You would act as a subcontractor supplying specialist writing services that the agency cannot handle.

Developing business sales
Development in business publishing means extending the number of projects you can handle for one client, or building up a group of clients either in the same industry or with similar requirements. Where you are working for just one client you need to decide whether it is better to be paid on an *ad hoc* basis for individual projects or whether it would be more profitable to be paid a retainer for providing an annual writing service.

You may find problems if you try to work for other companies in a similar business. Your clients may be competing directly or indirectly with each other for the same business; as a writer you are in a position to receive confidential information. To protect themselves some companies make you sign a confidentiality agreement, and insist that their suppliers do not work for competitors. However, there is nothing to stop you selling related writing experience to other non-competitive companies, so if you are supplying writing services to a computer manufacturer, you would be able to work for companies that supply software or manufacture data communications equipment. Your computer experience also gives you transferred electronics experience or, from an even wider viewpoint, experience of technical accounts.

A writing portfolio?

Portfolio is a term used by financial investors to describe a spread of different types of investment that yield a balance of short- and long-term returns, high, low and moderate returns, risks and safe bets, and protection. It makes a useful comparison with the writer's workload — a balance of long-term book income with regular short-term income from weekly or monthly magazines, low but regular returns from one magazine, to the occasional high earner.

Take a travel writer as an example. His long-term earnings could come from published travel books or from published guides to which he contributed. Regular or occasional income from newspapers or magazines would be based on freelance contributions, special supplements, or a regular column as an associate travel editor. Using a syndication agency he could get multiple sales from travel articles in the UK or overseas.

He also has established contacts with tourist boards and holiday operators. Twice a year he is heavily involved in writing copy for holiday brochures with tight deadlines to meet printing dates, and he also makes regular contributions to the various publications that the tourist boards issue. As his reputation is established he is invited to become a contributor to annual holiday and travel programmes on television: later, a full length television documentary on a country with which he is familiar.

Within that portfolio are projects that produce regular income — the weekly columns, regular special supplements, holiday programmes and holiday brochures. They give a good base for the other *ad hoc* projects, and the books help to establish a base for future years as royalties build up.

Writers who specialise in a 'domestic' topic, such as gardening, do-it-yourself, or cooking could expect a similar pattern in their portfolios, but in a market like sports writing, where there are competitive pressures from journalists as well as other writers, the balance could be different. To deal with the competition, a sports writer needs to develop areas of specialisation. Long-term book income could come from biographies — where the writer has exclusive access to interview material — or special interest sports. Regular income could come from monthly or weekly contributions to magazines dedicated to a particular sport, or as a special contributor backing up the team of general sports journalists on a newspaper. Television and video provide the opportunity for occasional high earning projects. Television programmes, such as the Channel 4 series introducing a wider variety of sports to the public, draw on the skills of specialist writers and presenters. Videos, demonstrating the skills in a sport, are produced by independent video companies working with specialist consultants and freelance writers.

The portfolio approach might seem relevant only to the work of a non-fiction writer, but it can also be applied to fiction. While full-length novels are likely to be the fiction writer's main form of activity, they are essentially long-term projects. A fiction writer needs the balance of regular short-term income. Magazines provide an opportunity in the form of short stories or serialised fiction, while radio has a variety of short story slots using material from new and established writers. Fiction competitions organised by newspapers or arts groups are the occasional earners in the portfolio. Book reviews and literary criticism can also provide occasional or even regular forms of income.

Whatever field you write in, you should aim to build up a portfolio like this as your experience and reputation grow.

If you want individual advice on developing your writing, contact The Writer's Portfolio Service, 51 Washington Road, Maldon, Essex CM9 6BN.

Changing direction

One of the most difficult tasks for a writer is to change direction. How can someone who has been writing magazine articles for ten years on a specific topic break out of that situation? It may be a question of survival — the demand for the articles on that subject may have declined dramatically — or it may be a deliberate choice — to explore new areas. The change may be a simple one — to write books rather than articles on the same topic — or it may involve a change of topic.

The section on a writing portfolio shows the wide variety of opportunities available within the same subject area. By applying the portfolio technique to your own chosen speciality, you can increase the scope and variety of your writing. The chapters that follow show opportunities and tasks that apply to different types of writing; you should study them carefully to make the most of the opportunities.

If, however, you wish to move outside a specialised area where you have had a degree of success, you need to have confidence in your ability to get work published. This is half of the formula for success — subject knowledge can be acquired through careful research, but the skills in producing work to publication standard are built up over a long period. Naturally, you may be able to transfer some of your subject knowledge to a new area, but this is less important than being able to write effectively for the reader.

Chapter 2

Magazines and Newspapers

Magazines

The number of magazines published in the UK grows every year. There are weekly, monthly and quarterly periodicals on every subject you can imagine. Every issue needs news and articles to fill the pages and satisfy the readers; it is unlikely that staff writers can meet all the demands. At least 600 general interest magazines use and pay for freelance contributions. That is only part of the story because there are 7500 periodicals published in the UK, of which the special interest magazines would use only expert contributions.

Of all the markets for freelance writers, magazines offer the greatest opportunities. Subject matter, length of article, rates of payment, frequency of publication — all vary between magazines and that means the writer can build up a good spread of work.

One important factor to remember is that only successful magazines can afford to pay good rates for articles. Success depends on attracting a quality circulation that will help them sell advertising space. Your articles will only be chosen if they appeal to that audience.

Magazines sounds like a homogeneous term, but the periodical market is very diverse. It is important to classify magazines to see where you should aim your work. The main distinction is between business and consumer publications — magazines for people at work or in private life. There is a further split into general interest and special interest magazines. The *Sunday Times Magazine* and *Woman's Own* are general interest consumer magazines; their equivalents in the business sector would be *Management Today* or *The Economist*. *Popular Gardening* or *Sinclair User* are special interest consumer magazines, while *Electronics Weekly* or *Pig Breeder* meets special interests in the business sector.

Information on freelance opportunities

There are a number of publications that give useful information on opportunities for freelance writers. *Writers' and Artists' Year Book* includes an alphabetical listing of magazines and their requirements and it also has a guide to the markets for items like fillers, readers' letters, short stories and subject articles.

British Rate and Data is a monthly publication that gives circulation details and advertising rates of magazines under a number of subject headings. It is used by the advertising industry to plan campaigns, but the information on readership is useful when you are assessing a magazine. *Willing's Press Guide* and *Benn's Media Directory* give even larger lists of periodicals including house journals and some of the more specialised publications. They add details of editorial staff and other important press contacts. These directories are expensive to buy, and are updated annually. You can, however, find them in your local reference library. For up-to-date information, *Freelance Writing & Photography* and *Contributor's Bulletin* give details of new magazines and point out other new opportunities.

The most useful form of research is field research, checking magazines in libraries or on bookshelves. You should look out for new publications or changes in individual style which could indicate a simultaneous change in editorial policy.

Staff and freelance contributors
Magazine copy comes from two main sources — staff and freelance writers. The contents page gives a clue to who's who. Under editorial staff are listed editors, staff writers and regular contributors. Anything that is not credited to them would be provided by freelance writers. There are also special contributors — the people who provide regular columns on subjects like health, law, motoring, travel and gardening.

The rest of the field is wide open, but it is worth checking the contents page to see whether the magazine accepts unsolicited material.

Copy length
You need to establish what length of article the magazine is looking for. Some of the magazines in *Writers' and Artists' Year Book* give this information but, for the rest, you have to rely on counting the words in a selection of articles for different editions. A pattern eventually emerges. A helpful editor will usually tell you the length he is looking for, and there may be considerable variation within a single issue. *Marketing*, for example, has a special features section which includes one-, two-

27

and three-page articles, each of a specified length. *Essex Countryside* is very specific, asking for 1500-word articles, while *Reader's Digest* is looking for articles up to 5000 words.

Copy dates

When you are planning a workload you need to know when copy is required and when payment is due. These dates depend on the frequency of publication, publication date and copy dates. Editors can advise you on copy dates and may give you a fact sheet that covers this type of basic information. A practical working guide would be six to twelve weeks ahead of copy date for weekly magazines, three to six months ahead for monthly magazines, and six to twelve months ahead for quarterly magazines.

If you plan to contribute to seasonal features in holiday, Christmas or Easter issues you will have to submit copy or proposals even earlier. There is a lot of competition to get material in those issues and the editors plan contents well in advance so that the advertisement department can take space bookings. It pays to be quick off the mark. If you study the editorial pattern of a magazine over a period of time you can work out the programme of special features and time your contributions to match.

In business publishing this is made easier by the editors, who publish lists of forthcoming features in advance. They can do this because they have a carefully defined audience. Many magazines are controlled circulation (they are sent only to named people and not sold to the public); the issues are planned to meet the needs of both readers and advertisers. Their published editorial programmes are ideal for planning work in advance, but check with the editors on a number of points. The editor may commission feature articles in batches, every six months for example, and may already have filled the spot you want. The lead times you have worked out won't be very useful then. Check also that the editor does not use the services of only one writer or editorial company to supply all copy for these features. There are companies who supply complete packages to magazines, writing and illustrating the editorial, and negotiating the advertising for the feature.

It's not always the staff editor who is responsible for special features. They may be handled by an outsider with a title like associate editor, or special features editor. Your material would normally be forwarded to the right person.

Readership and editorial content

Regular features and special features form the bulk of a magazine's contents. Other articles would be selected for their interest to readers. Knowing who these readers are is one of the writer's important tasks. The advertising in the magazine gives some clues. Magazines are set up to reach a particular target audience. The audience would be defined in terms of age, class, interests, and a number of other socio-economic factors. This breakdown is important not just for the information it gives to advertisers, but for the way it enables editors to tailor material for their readers.

British Rate and Data gives circulation details of most magazines, while many publishers produce their own readership surveys which break down the total circulation by category. Many business and technical publications are distributed on a controlled circulation basis to people who complete a registration form. This covers details of their jobs, responsibilities, company activities, and sometimes spending power. This information is incorporated into a media data form which is available to prospective advertisers. Readership surveys like this can be very useful to the contributor; they help to indicate the reader's likely interest.

It is the editors' task to decide the mix of articles. They look carefully at their audience, and their editorial decisions either reflect their readers' taste or attempt to create it. So it is important that you are in tune with the editors' view of what the reader wants to know.

Fiction in magazines

One of the biggest markets in women's magazines is the fiction market. There is a demand for serial fiction or single short stories. A number of magazines publish guidelines on length, style and the type of material they are looking for. D C Thomson, for example, who publish a large amount of fiction, positively encourage new writers and have prepared editorial guidelines for contributors.

Serialised fiction is not a homogeneous market. There are teenage, young adults' and children's markets and outlets for all age groups. Fiction, like magazine articles, should be aimed at a specific audience. This is a large and potentially lucrative market where a number of writers earn a good regular income. It doesn't always pay to be yourself though. A romantic pen-name is essential if you are writing fiction for women's magazines, and if you are a male writer hoping to succeed in that market, make the change quickly.

General articles

It's not what you write about that is important, but who you write it for. Sport, motoring, food, hobbies and crafts, interviews and profiles, travel, gardening, household, family — you find a similar pattern within most of the general interest magazines, but within those broad definitions the variation is enormous. The more adventurous the magazine, the more varied the contents.

That gives you, the contributor, a great deal of scope, but even if you are a subject expert you find plenty of outlets for your material. Financial columns, for example, can take a great many forms. There is a regular small saver's column in the *Financial Times, The Economist, Planned Savings, Money Management, Investors Chronicle, Money Minder, Financial Weekly, Daily Telegraph, Today, The Times, Daily Mail* and the Sunday newspapers. Motoring, holiday, travel, food, medical and gardening columns appear with the same sort of frequency and give you multiple opportunities for the same subject material. Often these columns are written by specialist writers who belong to accredited groups such as the Guild of Motoring Writers or the Guild of Travel Writers. You may find it useful to join one of these organisations if you intend to specialise in this area.

For the general writer *Reader's Digest* presents one of the most challenging opportunities. Editorial content is a mixture of new material that is contributed or commissioned, and material abridged from published sources. Its rates of pay are legendary, among the highest in the publishing business, and the rate for a joke or a letter is higher than many magazines pay for a full-length article. But the competition can be fierce. There is no limit to the sort of material that can be produced though the magazine has favourites such as hobbies, health, mental well-being and the wonders of nature. *Reader's Digest* should be on every good writer's list, not only for the wide-ranging opportunities it offers, but for the high editorial standards, and the excellent rates of pay.

Special interest magazines

The range of magazines that cater for special interest is growing rapidly. Sports, crafts, hobbies, do-it-yourself, motoring, and computing are just some of the major categories that you will find on newsagents' shelves. Here you are writing for an expert audience so specialised knowledge is essential. The rates of pay are likely to be lower than general consumer magazines but you have the opportunity to get material published more frequently. There are usually a number of magazines covering the same ground. If you are interested in writing on athletics you have a choice of *Athletics Weekly* and the monthlies — *Athlete's World*, *Marathon & Distance Runner*, *Today's Runner* and *Running* — as well as more general sports magazines such as *Sports Illustrated* or *Sports & Leisure*.

The newer leisure activities bring in their wake entire industries devoted to supplying the needs of the participants. The publishing business has not been slow to follow and there usually emerges a whole body of instructional and inspirational literature. One of the fastest growing sectors is computer magazines and there is now a vast range of consumer and business magazines. Unfortunately, much of the material that is published is not editorial — it is programs or instructions — but it does demonstrate the way in which markets can grow.

Business and technical articles
The trade press, as it is known, is an important part of the publishing business. Its role is to keep readers up to date with developments in their industry. In the carefully segmented, controlled circulation publishing operation that has developed, periodicals are aimed at people with a particular responsibility. In engineering, it could be the design engineer — specifying systems or components, but not necessarily buying them. In the same industry there are production engineers, maintenance engineers, electronics engineers, buyers and technical managers.

Technical magazines operate at a number of different levels. There are weekly news magazines, such as *Engineering Today*, which concentrate on topicality and business news. Monthlies like *Engineering* give authoritative coverage of developments within their industry, while journals like *Metalworking Production* concentrate on the specialised information that is relevant to their readers.

The editorial content is high on product news, new developments of interest, and business news. There are regular product surveys which look at particular supply industries, detailing all the suppliers and looking at new developments. Though much of the material originates with press releases from suppliers, the surveys also include a number of expert articles that are contributed by outside writers.

Instructional articles on services or products that are important but not widely understood are frequently published in trade magazines. They may be single articles or a series of articles covering a large and complex subject. Most technical magazines are very receptive to proposals for this type of project.

Technical journals tend to have a small permanent editorial staff and they are very helpful to freelance writers. As well as feature articles they are interested in receiving local news items. A good editor will send you a fact sheet outlining the sort of material he or she is looking for. This could include any topics that affect the trade, personnel news, appointments and promotions, manufacturing developments and investments. The fact sheet would also include the name of local contacts as well as copy dates and mechanical details.

Within each industry there are a number of magazines covering the same ground. They are not all directly competitive so the opportunities for reusing a subject are good. Rates of payment vary but are usually quite reasonable from the major trade publishing houses like Haymarket, Morgan Grampian or United Trade Press.

Partwork publishing

A very successful publishing development is the partwork magazine. Here a major subject is covered by a series of weekly or monthly magazines that build into a complete set. The medium has shown a remarkable ability to tackle virtually any subject – the Great War, knitting, the human body, gardening, and computing. If a subject is wide it stands a good chance of being partworked.

A partwork is coordinated by a series editor using a team of writers, designers and illustrators to work on specific assignments. The writers might be subject experts who work on their own specialist topics or might tackle a section of the whole project. The best known publishers in this field are Marshall Cavendish and Orbis who handle their own production. However, a number of partworks are produced by design and editorial consultancies who contract to put together a complete package. If you look at the credits in the magazine you can find out whom to contact.

Illustrated articles

Writing skill alone may not be enough if you are trying to sell to publications such as *Illustrated London News*, *National Geographic* or travel magazines. You need to cooperate with photographers and illustrators to succeed here. The *Traveller*, for example, recommends that an article of 3000 words should be accompanied by about 36 good colour transparencies and a selection of black and white photographs.

Photography or illustration can help to sell any article. The editor gets a complete package which needs no further attention. The photographs you supply may serve as a lead for another photographer; your photographs indicate the visual possibilities of the article. Not all magazines like their authors to supply photos; they may use staff photographers or commission others because they want to create a visual style for their magazine.

Newspapers

Newspapers still offer an important market for the freelance writer. On some newspapers closed shop arrangements (ie union labour only is used) mean little opportunity for the independent writer, but on other papers staff cuts create an increasing demand. There are three main types of paper — national, regional and local and they give different opportunities. *British Rate and Data* gives details of newspapers in these three classifications and you can get information on editorial staff from *Willing's Press Guide*.

Local newspapers

Local weekly newspapers are a good starting point; they have a demand for both reporting and feature writing skills. Because staff levels are usually low, the papers use freelances to cover one-off events, or to act as regular correspondents in their territory. If you have particular areas of knowledge — sport or industry, for example — you could act as a special contributor. Local papers publish feature articles on a whole range of topics of local interest, but the length is usually short, and payments comparatively low.

The editor is the main contact and he or she can supply you with a diary of events, addresses, contacts, and copy dates. News items for a local weekly are accepted up to two days before publication date, but you should allow several weeks if you are submitting feature articles. If you are working on a topical feature you should give adequate warning so that the editor can build this into the newspaper's schedule.

In many local newspapers regular feature articles such as the gardening, motoring or family doctor column are syndicated. The same article appears, often anonymously, in different newspapers, and this helps the editor to publish a comprehensive newspaper without employing a staff of under-used specialists. You can sell syndicated articles directly to groups of newspapers, or through a syndication agency.

Regional and national press

Regional daily and evening newspapers cover a larger geographical territory — a large town, part of a county or a region like East Anglia. The papers can be published as dailies or evenings, and include such famous names as the *Scotsman*, the London *Standard* and the *Sunday Post*. National newspapers such as the *Guardian*, *Sun*, *Today*, *Daily Telegraph*, *The Sunday Times*, *News of the World*, and the *Observer* are published daily or weekly, and are distributed throughout the country. Although the content of the nationals is, in theory, uniform throughout the country, there may be regional variations where different editions are printed in separate locations.

Local free sheets

An interesting new development is the local free sheet. These were regarded with suspicion when they first appeared in the 1970s, but they have since grown in respectability. Some indication of their development came in late 1984 when the Yellow Advertiser Group began to carry full colour on the front page, a feature that is still rare in the majority of newspapers. Originally they contained only advertisements, but now they are increasing their editorial content. Some of the editorial is related to advertisements but there are also short features of local interest and regular spots on gardening, motoring and sport.

A number of the free sheets are published by companies already producing traditional newspapers. They use a high percentage of common editorial and advertisements. Others are published by independents who specialise in free sheets, and issue a number of local editions. Free sheets have a very small editorial staff, and use outside contributors. However, they are delivered free (paid for by advertising), so there is little scope for large editorial fees.

Editorial staff

Your initial contact on a newspaper would be the editor, but on a larger newspaper the situation can be more complicated. The editor decides on the overall balance of the newspaper, but responsibility for individual sections lies with section editors who themselves write, and commission material from outside contributors. On a typical daily newspaper you might have editors for broad areas such as home news, international news, business, finance, sports, arts, women's section, travel, and education. Within those broad areas there would be special editors and contributors who concentrate on their own topics. The arts section, for example, might include book, theatre, film and television reviews, profiles of authors and performers, and general features on any of these topics. By looking at the bylines (attribution) on the articles, you can establish who is responsible and direct your contribution to the right people.

The byline normally includes the names of the writers, their responsibility on the publication — for example Jane Smith, Arts Editor — or the writers' qualifications if they are outside writers — for example Robert Jones, Director of the Arts Study Group.

Special features

Like magazines, newspapers publish occasional or regular special features in which a topic is covered in depth by a series of authoritative articles, and the feature is supported by advertisements. The *Financial Times*, for example, has an annual programme of surveys which deals with financial and business aspects of specific industries or overseas markets. *The Times* also publishes a regular programme of special reports covering similar ground.

The *Guardian* has regular weekly sections under headings such as Creative and Media, Education, and Futures which are a mix of news and feature material. Most newspapers publish occasional special features on holidays, travel and seasonal events. You can get information on a newspaper's advance programme of special features by writing to the advertisement department but for occasional features you need to build up a pattern by studying papers over a period of time.

35

Content and lead times

Feature articles in newspapers are generally shorter than magazine articles because of the greater emphasis on news. An average length would be 1000 to 1250 words, or perhaps less on some newspapers. Some newspapers indicate the length of article they are looking for, and you can get additional information from word counts in the newspapers themselves.

Copy dates and lead times vary from paper to paper. On regional newspapers editors prefer a week's notice for material that has to be published on a particular day, otherwise the article is published when space is available. Topical articles or 'calendar' articles should be planned well in advance. On national newspapers, where there is likely to be greater competition, you should allow for longer delays before publication. If you are contributing a regular feature you would be given a definite copy date to work to.

Chapter 3
Books

Some call fiction a dying sector but every year UK publishers manage to produce about 5000 new titles, and the news stories that capture public imagination continue to be the ones about the best selling novels that 'force' their authors into tax exile.

Fiction

The reality of the fiction book trade is that there are a lot of struggling authors earning very small sums of money for very good pieces of work. Author Frederic Raphael compared the thousands he received for his television series, *The Glittering Prizes*, with the sale of just several hundred copies of his previous novel, *California Time* — and he was an author of repute. Authors have to be prolific to survive, producing at least one book a year. Melvyn Bragg wrote nine books in nine years, Iris Murdoch 18 in 18 years and Simon Raven 14 in 15 years.

This is not to decry the quality or appeal of their work, or to suggest that they would not have written a book every year anyway, but it does suggest that slow writers will run into problems.

Certainly, the changed nature of the retail trade has not helped the novelist. Publishers are now more market-orientated. The large chain stores which dominate the buying of books apparently accept only fast turnover titles that have heavy promotional backing and are an attractive shelf proposition. This means that publishers must have confidence in their books to achieve that, and this must limit the chances of new authors.

At the same time, fiction produces very high earnings for authors whose books do succeed. Some of these books have to be rewritten by agents or ghost writers to give them a mass market appeal, a fact that is sometimes acknowledged by grateful authors, but not always mentioned.

New novelists
Large fiction houses reckon to receive over 1000 unsolicited

manuscripts a year, so the competition is fierce. But the possibility of one day finding the next bestseller means that few publishers will let a manuscript from a new author go without careful reading. They may even publish it, although it may not be a commercial success. Some critics say that new fiction is subsidised by the better selling books, and that many publishers are thus committing a kind of commercial suicide. However, they feel a responsibility for the future of good fiction, so it is likely that new fiction will continue to be published.

Library sales once made an important contribution to sales of new novels. Publishers used to reckon on an average of 1000 library copies which could account for almost 90 per cent of a book's total hardback sales, but with price rises and cuts in library expenditure, that number is down below 100.

Romantic fiction

There is one category of fiction that seems to sell well regardless of trade conditions — romantic fiction epitomised by publishers such as Mills and Boon, D C Thomson and Silhouette.

Articles about this type of fiction suggest that the authors make a reasonable living from it. Sales are high volume and turnover rapid, so the authors have to be prolific to keep up. Well-known authors talk in terms of writing four books a year, and of earning £15,000 to £20,000 per book.

New authors are encouraged, and published. D C Thomson send helpful comments on manuscripts, even if they don't accept them first time. To help new authors, the major publishers issue guidelines on the type of story they are looking for, giving an indication of characterisation, plots and events.

Subsidiary rights

As mentioned earlier, traditional fiction seems to be kept alive by publishers despite the efforts of the retail trade. But perhaps more important to the fiction writer than immediate trade sales with their low potential are the various subsidiary rights that are available — foreign rights, serialisation, and digest rights, film rights, and many other openings that can offer far greater rewards than the initial royalties.

Sales to book clubs, for example, are an important market for the fiction writer. A book club buys the right to publish a special edition of the book which bears its own imprint. It normally prints these special editions in large quantities, or takes a bulk supply from the publisher's print run, and can therefore offer readers a special low price as the members guarantee to purchase a stated number of books per year. The clubs promote their books in catalogues sent to members, and this publicity may be valuable in its own right. They generally undertake only books for which there is a hardback edition. The fee to publish book club editions is shared between author and publisher, and as clubs often buy copies at 75 per cent discount, it leaves little room for substantial royalties.

Paperback sales are another important source of revenue, but you have to make a number of decisions before choosing a publisher. If a publisher accepts your book and publishes it in hardback, he or she then takes around 50 per cent of the paperback rights which may be sold to a mass market paperback house. The value of the paperback rights has to be calculated carefully because one party is likely to lose out. A bestseller sold low leaves the publisher and author realising they should have asked for more. Because of the potential income from mass market paperback sales, many hardback publishers are willing to take on fiction that they know may even make an initial loss in hardback.

You could go directly to a paperback publisher but this has a number of disadvantages. As a rule, hardback books have a better chance of review (though with a bestseller this would be irrelevant) and many paperback publishers want to see a track record before committing themselves. You lose the opportunity of hardback sales with their higher royalty figure, and you may be unable to get your book published. Paperback publishers do not exist to put second-rate literature on the market; they aim to publish books that will sell in large quantities.

Foreign rights are sold to another publisher, who may be associated with the original one, to produce or market the book in other territories. It is normal for the original publisher to market the book in the 'traditional' territories which cover the Commonwealth and English-speaking markets, with the possible exception of the USA. Where books are translated into foreign languages, the local publishers usually bear the cost. They pay for marketing, producing and distributing the book, taking an income from sales, and paying a fee for rights (plus, usually, a royalty) which is shared between the original publisher and author.

Foreign sales can be very high and it can be the case that an author is better known overseas than in his or her own country. Nor is it uncommon for the UK's prohibitive tax laws to drive an author into tax exile. One very real threat to foreign sales is the piracy that is unfortunately becoming more common in markets in the Far East or Nigeria, for example. Here the original English version is reprinted and distributed cheaply, sometimes even reappearing in the UK, or it is translated into foreign languages without payment to the legitimate publisher.

All of these rights are built into a contract, and writers need to be aware of the clauses that affect them. Negotiating them can be a tricky business as Anthony Burgess found out when he was selling film rights for *A Clockwork Orange*. He sold the rights for a modest fee, and then saw the film makers change all his material, claim credit for the script, and make a lot of money out of it.

Fiction does not necessarily give the writer an automatic entry into the film world. The majority of writers have to live on royalty income, and the possibility that one day they might have a bestseller on their hands. Certainly, it is not possible to recommend what type of fiction is likely to be popular. Public libraries and some of the larger bookshops break fiction down into specific categories such as westerns, thrillers, spy, science fiction, romantic, historic, and other topics, but writing for these categories is no guarantee of success.

What is left of the market for short stories is concentrated in newspapers, magazines and competitions. Few books of short stories are published now despite their continuing popularity on radio. The full-time writer will probably need to supplement his income in other areas.

Non-fiction books

The market for non-fiction books is large, almost five times as large as for fiction. In 1986 just under 50,000 non-fiction titles were published, compared with 6000 fiction, and the value of non-fiction sales continues to rise. This is a healthy situation compared with fiction where bulk-buying policies by major retailers have reduced the variety of novels available on the shelves, cut traditional booksellers' margins and reduced total sales for all but the bestsellers. Gordon Wells in *The Successful Author's Handbook* pointed out that the Bible was the world's bestseller and that Paul Samuelson's *Economics* had sold several million copies.

Yet one of the most important markets for non-fiction has had its own problems in recent years. Educational books (see

Chapter 8) have suffered from cuts in school and college expenditure but they still maintain a healthy percentage of all non-fiction sold in the UK.

Non-fiction books have always formed an important part of the publisher's offering. The public library system was established in the nineteenth century to make widely available books of 'useful knowledge' that would help people to improve themselves. Fiction became a significant part of the library scene much later and non-fiction still forms a significant part of library stock.

The reader of a non-fiction book is looking for factual information to fill a gap in his or her knowledge, or for instructional information to give guidance on a particular subject. Your book should raise readers' levels of skill — help them to become a better tennis player, live a better life, or learn more about the life of Dickens. The text should be clear, logical and encouraging.

Non-fiction publishers
Most publishers carry a fairly long non-fiction list but they may specialise in particular non-fiction types and subjects. You can get more information by studying the bookshelves or looking through publishers' catalogues at the local bookseller.

Look particularly for series of books. That shows the publisher has an audience and market in mind, one that has been researched as being a profitable sector with good sales potential. Since a large part of the decision to publish depends on a book's sales potential, it will be easier for you to sell into an existing series. Part of the publisher's job has already been done. Your task then is to convince the publisher of the quality of your book, not of its sales potential. The only barrier is that the series may already be established and the publisher may not be planning any further titles. The single-shot book involves considerably more risk for a publisher, but if your book could form part of a new series, then it may be of more interest.

Book club and paperback opportunities are similar to those for fiction (see pages 38-40).

Book proposals
Before you write a non-fiction book there are several preliminary stages. To establish initial interest you don't need to write the entire text. In fact, few publishers want to receive a complete non-fiction book. According to them only about

1 per cent of unsolicited non-fiction manuscripts are eventually published. The publishers' initial task is to assess the market for the book and to do this they are more interested in an outline than the text. The publisher is not judging the quality of the book at this stage, so the author's real writing effort should come later. When the publisher has agreed the market for the book, an expert would read it to assess its contents. Only after this stage should you start writing the text. The content may have been substantially revised by this time.

Publishers vary in what they want to see in the initial proposal. Some prefer an introductory letter, followed by a synopsis if they are generally agreeable to the proposal. Other publishers lay down very firm guidelines, sending the author a pre-printed form, or new book proposal, which specifies the information they need. The content of these forms is a useful guide to what you should include in your proposal.

The publisher wants to know who the book is aimed at, and what the reader will gain; if you can quantify the audience so much the better; what competitors has the book got and why does your book make advances on previous published material; is the book suitable for educational and professional requirements?

The publisher also needs to know what length the book will make so indicate the anticipated number of words and state how many illustrations will be required. This helps to establish the cost of the book, and will also help the publisher work out a timetable for writing and publication. Your proposal can take the form of answers to a pre-printed questionnaire or a written document of your own that follows the same outline.

Research on the audience profile is important. It indicates the book's sales potential and it also shows that your book is not being written in a vacuum, or to satisfy a whim: it has a specific purpose and readership in mind. One of the questions in the proposal is about the book's potential for the educational market. You can get information by studying course syllabuses, exam papers and prospectuses. Books primarily intended for the education market are discussed in Chapter 8 but, for many non-fiction books, educational sales can be a valuable spin-off.

With the proposal you should send a detailed synopsis which sets out the structure and proposed contents of the book. The publisher uses this to assess the contents and, if necessary, get an expert reading. This is why few publishers want a complete manuscript as a first offering: they would have no opportunity to comment on the content and their advice can often help to improve the book.

The synopsis should include all the major topics to be covered. If you are preparing a book of say 50,000 words you should show how the book breaks down into sections or chapters (normally 10 or 12) and outline the main points of each. The synopsis helps you spot any omissions, duplication or imbalance in your plan.

The synopsis is not a straitjacket though. When you begin to write the text you may find the book going in a different direction. You will arrive at the same destination but the route may be very different. A publisher would probably not expect you to adhere strictly to a synopsis, but it is a necessary stage in planning the book.

What type of book?

There are many different types of non-fiction book, but they can be broadly classified into information and instruction books with a considerable overlap between the two.

Perhaps the easiest way to see the diversity of non-fiction is to study the library classification system. It divides books into broad categories such as sport, history or literature and then into further subsections such as football, cricket or climbing.

A very brief list of the types of books publishers are interested in would include art and literature, technology, science and management, sport, games, hobbies and crafts, biography criticism, medicine, natural history, philosophy and religion, travel and geography, politics and current affairs.

Before you begin working on a book, it is worth checking that you are not duplicating someone else's work. For example, in anniversary years there tends to be a great deal of effort put into commemorative editions or biographies that overlap and duplicate each other. The Arts Council of Great Britian offer a free service called 'Books in Progress'. This is a confidential information service where writers are asked to register any work they plan to carry out. They are advised whether anyone else is working on the same subject, so the scheme should prevent duplication and wasted work.

There is a great choice of work in non-fiction but some sectors of the market are growing at a faster rate and offer greater opportunities.

Instruction books

One of the fastest growing sectors in the instructional market is do-it-yourself. There now seems to be no limit on what an apparently unskilled, untrained person can tackle, given the right step-by-step guidance. Take building and home maintenance as an example. A look back to books of say 20 years ago shows the dramatic change in style. Then, when people tackled a home improvement project, they had to be reasonably skilled in bricklaying, plastering, know all the trade terms, and be familiar with all the techniques needed. Doing the job was a matter of following detailed instructions for a particular project, rather than learning the techniques as you went along. But all that has changed, and the emphasis now is on easy techniques and step-by-step instructions. This runs parallel with developments in home improvement retailing and people's willingness to tackle any project from rewiring a plug to major structural alterations, with extensions going up in every direction.

One of the pioneering works was the *Reader's Digest Complete Do-it-yourself Manual*, a two-part handbook covering techniques and projects. Do-it-yourself books have consistently raised the quality of presentation and set high standards of photography, illustration, and clarity of text. There are now books on almost every conceivable aspect of home improvement, yet there remain plenty of opportunities for new ones. The opportunities arise because books need updating to take account of new techniques, a job can always be done more simply, a book can be published to tie in with a television series, or a publisher may wish to extend his series or move into the market.

In this type of book collaboration with designers, photographers, and illustrators is essential. The production of major series of illustrated books is very much a team effort with an editor and art editor coordinating the whole project. But there is no reason why the individual writer should not operate in the same way, cooperating with other specialists. To achieve even greater clarity, publishers are introducing new techniques. One of the interesting variations is the pop-up book on do-it-yourself motor maintenance. Subject knowledge is clearly important in instructional books, but so too is the ability to think clearly.

The same principle of clear instruction can be applied to almost any subject such as gardening, knitting, or cooking. People are now practising hobbies or skills that would once have been the province of experts. Good publishing has contributed to that. One of the pioneers in this area was the Teach Yourself series which covered every subject from management techniques to sports and hobbies. They are still alive and well and extending their range but now they have more rivals.

Professional and technical books

Business education is another important publishing area — part of the category known as professional and technical publications. Professional textbooks aim to help their readers become better managers, or improve their marketing skills. They are a combination of case history, instruction and motivation, and they help people keep up to date with developments in their business. These are usually published in series, sometimes under the auspices of a professional body, such as the Institute of Marketing, or a newspaper — *The Times* Management Series is a good example. Some of the books are related to professional courses, helping people prepare for qualifications.

A major growth area in recent years has been books that show you how to set up your business — this book is part of such a series. They are aimed at people who have a technical, professional or personal competence in a certain area, and who now want to work for themselves. There are two types of book in this category — the general books cover the basic skills required to run any business while books like *Writing for a Living* cover one specific business in detail.

Your research should cover the existing publishers, looking at their range to see which occupations have not been covered and which could usefully be updated because of technological changes.

Although you need to have direct experience of the business to write with any conviction, you also need to write clearly, so there is a good case for collaborating with business professionals, managers or other specialists to get the best possible results.

Books on sport and leisure

Sport too has its body of improvement literature. There are teach yourself books which cater for people of different standards and participation is no longer limited to the experts. Perhaps the most obvious example is marathon running. Once an élite sport which attracted only a handful of seasoned athletes, it now attracts millions of runners in the mass participation events like the London Marathon for which some 80,000 people apply every year. The boom started in the USA several years ago before it came to the UK, and it brought its own literary style. The literature is in the inspirational style — you can do it, you can overcome it — and the message is proclaimed with almost evangelical fervour. But the books also contain practical advice on clothing, training, eating and dealing with injuries. Running books have proliferated and their popularity has grown with the boom. They are written by athletics coaches or by successful runners who have retired, often in collaboration with professional writers. Running books are improving; they are usually well illustrated with photographs and diagrams, but they haven't yet reached the coffee table standard.

Although few sports can claim to have attracted the audiences that marathon running has, there is a growing interest in all forms of sport and leisure. Often the booms are fuelled by television or other media. Aerobics and snooker are two examples of leisure activities that have rocketed as a result of television coverage and created entire industries. Darts is enjoying the same sort of boom, though jogging seems to need little support from television. Not all booms last though — remember skateboards or the Rubik cube. There is a risk in any boom that it will be short-lived, so your own investment in time in a book could be wasted if you can't react fast enough. The problem doesn't just rest with the author.

For the publisher to get a book on the shelves quickly, before the start of the sport's new season, it takes some very careful planning and a lot of rush work. Topical books are hard to justify unless there is very large sales potential for the first book on the market. The whole process of writing, editing, setting, proof-reading, printing, selling and distribution has to be compressed. Inevitably there are overtime costs and risks of error. And public taste is fickle.

The other important type of sports book is the biography of famous sports personalities, written either while they are still famous or after they have retired. It used to be the practice to write memoirs after retirement, but with sportsmen in many fields now becoming media personalities, it is common to find biographies appearing while they are at the height of their careers. Sometimes they write their own biographies but, if they are not writers, there is either a ghost writer in the background or the book is written in collaboration with a sports journalist.

Occasionally sports biographies are written without reference to the sportsmen at all — by an observer. They might be based on press clippings or a series of interviews with other observers. It is unusual but it happens.

There is a whole range of commemorative books — football annuals, the book of the Olympics, or the golfer's year-book — which are usually compilations of factual information, records and results, and theme articles contributed by observers or sports personalities. The records and results are added late in the production process to keep them up to date, but the theme articles would be commissioned and written earlier because they vary in length and need editing to suit the space available. You should contact the editors soon after publication of the current issue, because they will already be working on the next one. For your contribution you would be paid a fee rather than a royalty because you are only part of a team.

Reference books
As well as writing complete books on your specialist subject you can also contribute to reference books or encyclopaedias. Compilation sports books were one example, but this is a very broad field and you should use your reference library as a source of information on the opportunities available. The publishers would use expert contributors coordinated by an editorial team so you should register your interests and skills with the publishers at an early stage. They are likely to be working on new editions continuously so you can never predict the right time to contact them. A check on the list of contributors to a reference book will indicate the number and calibre of people they use. If the list shows that every contributor is a university professor and you are not, then don't bother.

Working in non-fiction
This brief look at different types of non-fiction books shows the diversity within each field. You can apply the same principles to other areas. There are books for different levels of reader, compilation books, reference books, instruction manuals, and heavily illustrated books sometimes known as coffee table books. Non-fiction is likely to be a major part of any writer's output.

Children's books
Children's books form a well-defined section of the total book

market. In the last 30 years more than 60,000 children's books have been published. By 1979 some 24 million children's paperbacks had been sold, and there were over 6000 special children's bookshops in schools. The Book Trust (previously the National Book League) publish a list of children's books and they also run a children's reference library. You can get information on the publishers of children's books from publishers' catalogues or the reference books listed in Chapter 15.

Age groups
There is no single children's category. The books are divided by age for both fiction and non-fiction, and the main categories are pre-school, children's, teenage, and young adults. Each group has different needs, and you should bear this in mind. Publishers make the point strongly, and when you submit work you should specify the age group you are writing for. A simple distinction could be small, medium and large children. The small group, up to eight years old, is new to reading; the medium group is 8 to 15, and the young adults are from 15 upwards.

Educational requirements
Good publishers of children's books are aware of their educational responsibilities to their readers. Educational books are dealt with in Chapter 8 but the comments on style and language apply equally to all books for young readers. Some of the larger publishing houses, such as Ladybird, have a consultant educational adviser to guide authors, while others supply word lists for basic vocabulary books. Although these are not educational books in the strict sense, they are written to help children learn so it is important that standards are high.

Illustrated books
Books for the younger age groups can carry as much illustration as text. That doesn't mean you have to be an illustrator, nor do you have to suggest someone to do this. Publishers prefer to brief their own illustrators because they can give them specific instructions about subject, treatment, artwork requirements, and budget restraints. Illustrators visit publishers regularly to show samples of their work, and they use agents to keep in touch. You have the opportunity to comment on the illustrations, so it is not completely out of your control.

Subjects for children's books
The subjects for children's books are unlimited, and the

comments made on fiction and non-fiction books also apply here. There are a number of well established series that show which topics are popular — adventure stories, mysteries, did-you-know books, how to series, and reference books of all types. It seems there is always room for another 'Famous Five' or *Life in Tudor Times*.

Other markets for children's books

Television and radio companies use published books or extracts from them in children's programmes. For this they pay a broadcasting fee which is shared between author and publisher. Sometimes a programme producer will commission a new story or book from an author for broadcasting, and then subsequently publish the material under a special imprint, such as the 'Jackanory' series.

There is also a large number of annuals, children's magazines, and children's sections of general magazines that accept stories and articles.

Chapter 4

Radio and Television

According to *Writing for the BBC*, BBC Radio is the biggest employer of writers in this country. It broadcasts over 500 hours every week and the opportunities are greater than in television. There are four national radio networks covering the whole country, with regional variations, and at community level there are local BBC and independent radio stations. In addition there are the broadcasts of the BBC External Services and the BBC World Service.

Radio

Details of radio stations, their policies and the programmes are given in *Writers' and Artists' Year Book*, *Writing for the BBC*, the *BBC Annual Report*, *IBA Yearbook* and various media directories. Information on radio programme content appears in the *Radio Times*, *TV Times*, and the *Listener*.

If you are submitting material to network radio you need to contact the right department, so it is important to understand the organisation. The main departments in BBC Radio are Drama, Light Entertainment, Talks and Documentaries, Music, Radio 1, Radio 2, Outside Broadcasts, and Current Affairs. Network controllers are responsible for the mix of programmes that are broadcast on the four networks, but the mix is determined by submissions from different departments. Your point of contact should be the producer within a department.

The unique feature of writing for radio is that you have the opportunity to broadcast your own material on one of the many talks programmes. This can be a good lead into other opportunities such as contributions to magazine programmes, material for light entertainment, scripts for documentaries or for drama. The BBC Radio Script Unit is a useful source of information. It issues a leaflet on general requirements and standards, and will advise writers on the BBC's forthcoming requirements.

Talks

Radio talks on the BBC are produced by two departments — Talks and Documentaries, and Talks and Current Affairs. Talks are normally fairly short — 5, 10 or 20 minutes — and if you pass the microphone test you can read out your own talk. A five-minute talk read at average speed would consist of about 200 words. There appear to be no limits on the subject you can talk about, though *Writing for the BBC* gives guidance on what is not wanted. As an example they suggest that talks on travel are popular provided they can be presented in an interesting way, but holiday reminiscences are out. Biography is also suitable for talks.

The Talks and Documentaries Department is also responsible for programmes on arts, science and current affairs. Programmes on these topics frequently use talks of up to 20 minutes. You should submit these initially as an outline to the programme producer.

An extension of the basic talk is the interview. In the studio the set-up is no more complicated than a table, chairs, and microphones. If you are interviewing outside the studio you need good recording equipment.

Radio news

Radio news can be a useful course of work because both local and national stations and news agencies use news from local correspondents. They need immediacy, someone on the spot, so you must be able to get your material into the station quickly. Writing for radio news takes special skills. With an average news bulletin lasting 10 minutes or less, individual items would probably last no more than 40 seconds, unless they were major stories. That means a maximum of about 100 words of text, so the ability to write concisely is important.

As well as supplying pure news items you can also contribute interviews and background feature material for the more extended news broadcasts. Each broadcast of the material in different form would earn a separate fee.

Features and documentaries

News items and talks are a good starting point for the radio writer but you don't always have to broadcast your own material. Radio uses a mix of complete programmes and short items from freelance writers. Magazine programmes, for example, like 'Woman's Hour', include talks and feature items by staff and freelance writers. The Drama Department produces literary and feature programmes in addition to its drama output. There are also regular current affairs programmes that use a mix of material. The BBC recommends that you send an initial outline before submitting complete scripts.

Documentary programmes on current affairs or dramatised features on literary or historical subjects share certain characteristics. They combine narrative with other techniques such as interviews, voice overs, sound effects and music. Documentaries like 'Fishing the Herring' broke new ground when they were first broadcast, using a combination of narrative, traditional ballads and interviews in a piece of innovative radio. For a documentary programme you should first submit a rough synopsis and, on approval, prepare a full synopsis with some pages of sample script.

Drama
Radio drama, like its television counterpart, offers good opportunities for new writers. The Script Unit directs the manuscripts it receives to the most suitable producer, and takes an interest in encouraging new writers. The Unit publishes a pamphlet 'Notes on Radio Drama' and invites promising writers to discuss their work.

New writers have to submit a full script for a play; only established writers can submit ideas in synopsis form. Plays for Radio 4 should be written to the length of the programme you are aiming at. Currently there are a number of opportunities. 'Afternoon Theatre' broadcasts three 45-minute plays each week. There are two 90-minute plays each week: the 'Monday Play' and 'Saturday Night Theatre', and there is a weekly serial broadcast on Sunday evenings. Radio 3, according to *Writing for the BBC*, accepts plays of any length and nature so long as they are of a high standard.

The material needed for these programmes can be original plays written specially for radio, or they can be adaptations of existing material — novels or perhaps short stories.

Light entertainment
The Light Entertainment Group is responsible for comedy and variety programmes. You can either contribute material for existing programmes or submit ideas for new programmes or series. Some of the review programmes use sketches and jokes from a variety of sources, and you should send these directly to

the producer of the programme. Situation comedy, on the other hand, is written by the writer or team who devised the programme.

If you want to put forward material for a new programme or series you should start with a synopsis and sample script but you will eventually need to produce complete scripts before the idea can be finally assessed.

Local radio

Local radio is a comparatively new phenomenon. The first stations were in part a response to the demand that was demonstrated by the pirate radio stations of the 1960s. The programme content is very different, though. While the pirate stations were broadcasting almost continuous pop music, local radio is a mix of material — news, music, features, special interest spots and talks — as well as regular sports reviews and news of local activities. Its aims are to provide a local information service as well as entertainment.

Both the BBC and IBA operate local radio stations. The total number is currently about 70 and they are all looking for material of local interest. In some cases the stations ask for contributions from local writers only. They also have fairly low budgets, so if there is any payment at all, it is likely to be small.

You can get details of programmes from local newspapers, *Radio Times* or *TV Times*, and you should send material to the station editor or programme editor.

Fees for radio material

Fees for radio are calculated at a rate per minute broadcast. The rate varies with the type of material and the status of the writer, ie new or established. If the material is commissioned, payment is in two parts, half on commission and half on acceptance, but if you submit material you get payment on acceptance.

These are the fees for first broadcast, but there are additional fees for repeats, sale of transcriptions of your material, and fees for broadcast of the material overseas.

Writing for television

Writing for television is widely regarded as the most exciting form of writing and the one that offers the greatest rewards to your reputation and finances. While it is true that more than a million people may be watching the play you have written, few of them will remember your name. When the credits roll over the screen your name is just one of many. Although that programme would have had no existence without your script, your name is no more prominent than those of the actors, technicians and production staff.

Anonymity does little to reduce the attraction of writing for television. There are only a small number of writers whose work appears regularly on television, yet the BBC is the biggest employer of writers in the UK. That means the opportunities for freelance writers to break in are good. Certainly the television companies encourage new writers, but one success does not lead to a regular flow of work. The only regular work in television is series work, and that is usually handled by the professionals with proven experience of delivering scripts under pressure.

But television is more than series; every week there are over 200 hours of television on four channels, and each year the BBC broadcasts more plays than are produced in the West End. The writer's task is to identify the people who are buying the scripts and provide the right sort of material.

Unfortunately, writers are not always credited at the end of the programme, but careful research in *Radio Times* or *TV Times* helps you to identify programmes that use writers. Magazines like the *Listener* discuss programmes in considerable detail and there are programmes like 'Did you see?' which discuss programme making and often feature writers. Sometimes there appears to be no writer on the programme; this would indicate that there is a staff writer who prepares the script, or that the producer or director has written the material. Day-to-day research is the best way to find out what the writing opportunities are, but there is an introductory guide in *Writing for the BBC* which outlines the Corporation's main requirements.

The book's main message is that to look for opportunities you need to be aware of the structure of the BBC. It is not the BBC that is looking for scripts: it is individual departments, and their requirements vary enormously. Finding the right person gives your script a better start. The same principle can be applied to Independent Broadcasting Authority (IBA) companies though the structure is different. Here there are a number of regionally based programme contractors, and in theory each one could be buying the same types of scripts. In practice they tend to specialise in particular types of programme and their departmental structure would reflect the emphasis. There are also independent programme makers who supply material to both the BBC and IBA companies and their numbers are likely to grow with the coming of cable television.

Networks and regions

Programmes for the BBC and IBA can be broadcast on the complete national network or in the regions. Network programmes reach a larger audience and command a higher fee, but the existence of regional programmes gives the writer more than one opportunity to have his work accepted. If you are offering scripts to IBA companies you have as many opportunities as there are regions.

The BBC makes the majority of its programmes for network transmission in London but regional production centres at Bristol, Manchester and Birmingham also contribute programmes to the network. Other national production centres at Cardiff, Belfast and Glasgow make programmes for the Welsh, Northern Ireland and Scottish networks. The pattern of BBC broadcasting is that all regions receive network programmes for the majority of viewing hours but, for a certain period each day, they opt out of the network and have programmes with a regional flavour.

There is some overlap between the programmes made by the regions and the network centres, so material that was rejected by central departments might be taken up by a regional producer. If your material has a strong regional flavour, then it is more sensible to start in the regions.

BBC Wales and BBC Scotland also encourage authors who wish to write in Welsh or in Gaelic. They broadcast drama and current affairs programmes and you can find details of these in *Radio Times.*

IBA broadcasts have a more pronounced regional pattern. The contractors contribute programmes for network broadcasting, but much of their output is for regional broadcast only. If you studied all the regional editions of *TV Times* for a particular week you would see the variation in programme balance. Unless your script has a strong regional interest you can start with any contractor.

Television departments

BBC or IBA, regional or network television, whatever company you are aiming at, it is important that you contact the right department within the company. Both BBC and IBA companies have central script units that can channel your work to the right department in the first place. The BBC's TV Central Script Unit receives some 10,000 unsolicited scripts each year, so it pays to be very specific in aiming your material at a department.

The major departments in the BBC are Drama, Light Entertainment, Current Affairs, Science Features, Music and Arts, Children's Documentary Features, and Outside Broadcast. The balance of programmes broadcast by the different departments is initially decided by the network controller. The decisions are based on offers made by the departments; the offer is a proposal to make a programme together with an indication of likely production costs.

Producers

Your point of contact within this process is the individual producer. Producers are the people who put together the offers, and eventually the programmes that result from a successful offer. They are some of the most important people in the television process, and the BBC constantly stresses the autonomy and importance of its producers. They are responsible for commissioning scripts, casting and budgeting programmes. You or your agent should send your material to the producer of a particular programme. If it is a new idea or proposal, you should go through the Central Script Unit. Although the producer is always the ultimate contact, the opportunities and the methods of submitting proposals vary within departments.

Plays

Drama offers untried writers the biggest opportunities. The BBC broadcasts more plays each year than all of the West End theatres together, putting on more than 400 drama productions each year.

Television drama takes a number of different forms — there are individual plays produced under the umbrella of a series like 'First Love', and series or serials. Individual plays vary in length from 30 to 75 minutes and the most likely starting point for a newcomer is a 50-minute play. Some series of plays are written solely by newcomers. Channel 4, for example, encourages new talent and some of the BBC regions put together series of plays by new local talent.

Plays for television can be original plays, adaptations of other plays, or dramatisations of novels or other material. Before you adapt material you have to be sure that the rights are available.

Dramatisation is a particular skill, and the television companies tend to rely on experienced writers. For that reason new writers should begin with original plays.

As a first stage you should submit a brief outline and a few pages of sample script. What you are trying to sell is an idea that is dramatically interesting and can be produced within a reasonable budget, ie, without too many sets, actors, or changes of location. If this initial proposal is acceptable you would be asked to complete the script. If you are an established writer the idea can be commissioned on the synopsis alone, but if you are a new writer you need to complete the script before the idea can be accepted. The completed script also has to be 'satisfactory'. If the producer does not accept it then he has the option of bringing in another writer, and you could lose the final part of your payment.

Part of the process is knowing the language of television and making the best use of the medium. If you are not familiar with television scripting techniques and the technical aspects of production you can improve your knowledge from practical courses, or from courses run by correspondence schools. As the play gets further into the production process, the script will develop and change to take account of the practicalities of production. It goes from an initial reading script, through rehearsal scripts, and finally to a production script with all the director's instructions incorporated.

Drama series and serials

The only problem with writing a play is that once it is broadcast you have to wait for the next opportunity, and that could be a long wait. There are few opportunities for regular work except in series and serials, and then producers prefer to use experienced writers who can be relied on to deliver scripts regularly, sometimes providing seven or more scripts in advance.

A serial is one continuing story, broken down into episodes. It might be a finite story, adapted from a book, which ends in episode 13, or it may be an open-ended serial which continues for years, sometimes with a seasonal break. 'Jane Eyre' and 'Dallas' are examples of the finite and open-ended serials respectively. A series may have a similar time span, but each episode would be a self-contained story. 'Dempsey and Make-peace' and 'Minder' are examples of long-running crime series. The central characters are the same, and the situations may be similar from episode to episode, but each weekly story has a beginning and an end.

If you are proposing a series or serial, you need to prepare a 'format'. For a serial you should show how the story breaks conveniently into episodes, allowing for commercials on ITV or Channel 4, and indicate how many episodes there will be. The television year divides naturally into the four seasons, so many serials are based on a 13-week span, but there are also four- or six-week units. A new phenomenon in recent years is the 'blockbuster' serial which concentrates a long story into very few episodes. Each episode could last up to several hours, and the whole story may be broadcast over a short period like a week or a bank holiday weekend. You also need to show how many main characters will appear during the course of the serial and include some sample dialogue.

A series could be broadcast for similar periods of time. What you need to show in your proposal is that your characters, themes and situations have the potential to create a continuing series of stories for the first, and any subsequent series. You need to discuss the length and number of episodes, the main characters, types of situation, and include some sample plots.

Another form of proposal is the 'telenovel', a book that makes an easy transition from novel to television serial. Frederic Raphael's *The Glittering Prizes* and Malcolm Bradbury's *The History Man* were both moderately successful as novels, but translated readily into popular television series, earning their authors television fees equal to, if not better than their book royalties. Sales of novels are dramatically improved by successful television adaptation. In each case, book sales leapt during the transmissions.

The books divided into sections that equated with television episodes in length, there was a core of central characters, and the text contained large amounts of dialogue which formed an immediate basis for the actors' scripts.

If your proposal for a series or serial is accepted you may be invited to write all the episodes. Because of the pressure to have a number of scripts ready in advance, producers prefer to use experienced writers, and sometimes to spread the load. However, if it is your idea that is accepted, you will be paid a royalty for each episode broadcast. At the end of the programme you may see the credit 'created by'; this shows that the person who proposed the series and the writer of that episode are two different people.

When separate writers are used the procedure is that producers contact writers or their agents with the series format and evaluate their proposals before commissioning individual episodes. Their decision depends as much on experience and availability as writing skills; it is not unusual for a new writer to be given the opportunity to write one episode of an established series, but only to be paid if the script is acceptable.

Light entertainment
If drama is the lifeblood of television writers, it is not the only source of work. The Light Entertainment Department of the BBC and its IBA equivalents produce comedy and variety programmes. Entertainment programmes whether they are situation comedies, quiz shows or celebrity programmes need scripts and ideas. Someone has to devise the idea and formula for a quiz show, even though the script requirements are minimal. The revue type of comedy show uses sketches, jokes and continuity material supplied by outside writers — witness the long lists of contributors that appear in the credits to these programmes. To find out the current programme requirements you can contact the comedy departments of the BBC or IBA contractors.

The scripts and ideas for situation comedy series are normally created by one writer or by a single team. The proposal for a series is similar to the drama series 'format': you should include the number and length of episodes, the main characters, and a selection of situations together with a sample script.

Other departments
Television's other output includes current affairs, music, arts, science, sport, and general features. There are opportunities for freelance writers within these areas, but not so clearly defined as for drama or light entertainment. In departments like Music and Arts or Documentary Features, staff writers or programme producers write their own scripts, using expert contributors to supply much of the content. However, there is no reason why you should not submit a proposal for an item or an entire programme.

Cable television and independent contractors
It isn't just the BBC and IBA contractors who make programmes for the broadcasting companies. Television may not be their only activity; they may be film producers or an animation

studio, but they do represent a source of work for script-writers. The magazine *Contacts* lists these companies and their activities.

Cable television is an established part of the American television scene, but in Britain it is currently at the planning stage. It is not clear how great an opportunity this will present for production companies, and subsequently writers.

In theory, cable will allow subscribers to receive specialist programmes that relate to their own interests. This would seem to represent an opportunity for a wide spread of minority interest programmes, but early indications are that the financial arrangements do not allow for a great deal of programme making, so repeats and ready-made programmes will be prominent. But cable is at an early stage, and that could change. The initiatives are likely to come from the independent programme makers.

Chapter 5

Feature Films

This chapter is concerned with feature films on general release and not with sponsored films which are discussed in Chapter 6.

Opportunities

To go on general release a film does not have to be a Hollywood great, or even an Elstree production. Independent film makers who get the right financial backing produce films for general distribution. The script-writer can start at many different levels.

Film scripts can have their origins in many different sources. They can be adaptations of novels or plays, or they can be original stories for film. Though they might start as stories in words, they have to be turned into screenplays where the visual element is as important as the words. Action and settings have to be built into the script, then camera instructions, until your original script becomes a director's working document.

A script is not complete until it has been through the hands of many other people. Scripts are not for publication as they stand; they are part of the whole film making process. A screen-writer needs to know all about the various stages of filming.

Selling scripts

Where to go with a good script? Unless you are a full-time screen-writer, you are unlikely to have any ties with a production company. Agents are useful sources of work and market information; they know who is looking for scripts and they are in regular contact with producers. Agents consider proposals from new writers, but they prefer to represent established writers who have successfully delivered scripts. Their charge is normally 10 per cent of the fee.

If you are a newcomer you can send your proposal to an agent or directly to the story department of a production company. Kemp's *Film and Television Yearbook* is one of a number of directories that list production companies and independent producers. What you are selling them initially is an idea, one that catches the imagination, but one that is also practical within a budget. Films are expensive to produce and the people who finance them want to make a profit.

The ideal proposal would contain a package of script, production team, principal members of the cast and a budget. Budgeting is not the writer's direct concern but your script can make a contribution. You need to know about the stages of production and the way in which they can affect a budget. This would include the projected shooting time, the size of the crew needed, the number of locations and size of the cast, and the number of sets required. This gives the producer a basis for calculating budgets.

Developing a script

If your proposal is accepted it will go through a considerable number of changes before emerging as a film. The normal progression would be story outline, treatment, screenplay and various levels of shooting script.

The *story outline* is the preliminary planning stage where an idea becomes a story. The script acquires a basic structure and the writer can assess the amount of research still to be carried out.

The *treatment* is the stage where the writer adds more detail about characters and location, sequence and timing. By now other people may be making a contribution, and the next stage in the process — the screenplay — will involve a lot of cooperation. The *screenplay* is the document that shapes the way the film is made and you need to work with a director. You need to establish locations, discuss dialogue and characters, and assess technical problems before shooting.

At this stage the writer becomes part of a team and the script is shaped by input from producer, director, actors, cameramen, special effects people and technicians. The script may develop as shooting progresses, and the whole film can change again when it is edited in the cutting room. So it is important, if you are writing for the screen, that you understand the technical aspects of film making and are aware of the visual possibilities of the medium. Some of the great screen-writers have been directors as well — people like Ingmar Bergman who talked of the total team effort that went into his films. He was writer, producer and director, and his scripts were conceived as total entities from the start.

The screenplay becomes a technical document before shooting begins. The director prepares a *shooting script*, which is the screenplay plus all the camera and technical instructions, and this guides the rest of the production process. Wolf Rilla compares the screenplay with a map — the director should not lose his way to his destination, but he should be able to take alternative routes.

The script is read and used by many people so it must be clear in its instructions, and it should follow script writing conventions. Books like Wolf Rilla's *The Writer and the Screen* discuss the mechanics of script writing. They tell you how to lay out scripts, what different types of instruction mean and describe the processes of shooting and editing. The Writing School runs a correspondence course which includes film script writing techniques in its syllabus.

There are a number of basic conventions that you should follow. Included in the screenplay should be a description of characters, details of action, motivation and behaviour. For each scene you should indicate location, duration, details of buildings or other sets and any special effects. You should indicate the point at which the scene changes and number each scene consecutively. To separate dialogue from the rest of the script material, you should leave a line space and indent the material from the left. You don't have to separate single elements on the left and right side of the pages.

AUTHOR: You should leave a line space and indent material

from the left.

Fees and contracts

The Writers' Guild is pressing for a minimum agreement with the Film Producers' Association but at this stage there are no minimum terms.

Chapter 6

Writing for Audio Visual

Audio visual (or A/V) is a growing business. Companies use slides, film and video to create sales, marketing, training and financial presentations for employees, customers and visitors. In education and training, audio visual continues to play an important role. And in the domestic market the use of video and video disc is creating another form of leisure publishing.

The term 'audio visual' covers a number of different media including slide-tape, filmstrip, multi-screen or multi-media, films, video and video disc. All of them offer opportunities to writers, though it is difficult to pinpoint the sources of work.

Slide-tape programmes

Slide-tape is the most widely used audio-visual technique. At its simplest it is a do-it-yourself medium but it can get very sophisticated. A series of single images on 35mm slides is projected on to a screen, and the accompanying commentary is pulsed to change simultaneously with each slide. A programme would last 10 to 20 minutes or longer and, in a single projector show, would consist of a maximum of 80 slides (the maximum capacity of a rotary slide magazine). The pulse that changes the slides is electronic — a signal recorded on to one track of a twin-track tape recorder.

The writer's job is to create a script that provides a commentary for the image on the screen or explains it. There are a number of mechanical skills to learn. You have to work out the duration of the commentary with a stop watch and then put a pulse on the tape where the change should occur. The pulse and the commentary have to take account of the length of time it takes a slide to change, ie the mechanical ability of the projector. While a slide is changing the screen is dark, perhaps for several seconds, so it is important not to have the commentary starting too soon.

The single projector slide presentation is the simplest form of scripted audio visual. It can be used for all the main types of presentation, but its limitation is that there is only one single image on the screen at any time.

Twin projector slide-tape

A more sophisticated version of slide-tape uses two projectors with a dimmer control between them. What happens is that one image on the screen is lighting up while the other is fading down. The system is known as cross-fade projection and it has the potential for a whole range of creative effects. As one image blends into the other on the screen you can make comparisons between successive images and dissolve one image into the other to create the impression of continuity or change. By modifying the speed of change it is possible to add more elaborate effects. These creative effects help you to explain and clarify complex subjects. When you are planning your script you should make use of the whole range.

The commentary is recorded on tape with a pulse track. The pulse track is more complicated this time because the change is not simply a mechanical one, but creative.

Multi-screen presentations

Even more advanced presentations can be created with three or more projectors controlled and programmed by computer-based units that can create extraordinary special effects. As the equipment gets increasingly complicated the presentation becomes almost theatrical — multi-media shows where film, audio and slide-tape are used together to create an 'experience'. Sometimes as many as 30 projectors are used and the show becomes a piece of technical wizardry.

The theatrical shows are often used as a kind of exhibition and they are found in museums, tourist centres and at other major events around the world. The Beaulieu Motor Museum and Singapore Experience are examples.

Filmstrips

Filmstrip is closely related to slide-tape. Individual images are printed on a single strip of film and projected in sequence. Some filmstrip projectors have the facility to replay a commentary on tape, but the majority have no facilities for sound. There are systems on the market that can synchronise pictures and commentary. They come in a carrying case and the images are projected on to an integral screen. Programmes last up to 25 minutes and consist of a maximum of 180 pictures.

This development has taken filmstrip from its primitive beginnings to a reasonably compact and reliable system of projection which is very portable. Company salesmen use them to demonstrate their products in the customers' own offices or to train people in the field, away from a formal training environment. One of the largest users is the medical supplies industry which uses filmstrip to demonstrate new products to busy doctors in the surgery.

Speaker support slides

It isn't always necessary to have a recorded track to change slides in the projector. With a fairly simple set-up — say up to three projectors — this can be done manually while the speaker performs live. The writer's task here is to edit the presenter's speech or script so that it works with the slides. You have to work closely with the speaker to make him aware of the intervals when the slides change. By modifying the text to allow for creative changes, you can get the best effects from cross-fade projection. Live speakers are less predictable than pre-recorded tapes because they can forget their words, lose their place or sneeze, and the slides end up out of sync. It is a challenge, and it can be very satisfying.

Working with audio-visual specialists

The more complicated the projection system the more likely that a pre-recorded tape will be used. The writer's task is the same whatever the level of sophistication — to reinforce the visual message — but the higher the technology, the greater the need to cooperate with people who understand it and know how to achieve the most creative results.

In all the programmes you need to work closely with designers, photographers, speakers and producers. An audio-visual programme is a joint production. Initially you can use your own basic projector and recording equipment to plan the programme but for the final sound track you will be working with sound recording engineers, sound effects people and perhaps actors.

66

Opportunities for freelance script-writers

Audio-visual programmes have many roles and the scripts operate at different levels. If you are writing scripts you work to a specific brief — you are not offering a script for publication or broadcasting. The work can come from a number of sources and you need to keep in regular contact so that you are considered when there is a script to write.

Large companies may have the resources to produce simple programmes internally. They own or hire projection equipment and put together their own programmes using outside studios to supply artwork or slides. Companies in the financial sector, for example, produce a large number of slide presentations to explain the effects of fiscal changes or introduce new products. Production of the programmes can be the responsibility of the publicity department, training department or marketing department.

The same departments might use outside suppliers to conceive and produce the entire programme. They include advertising agencies, design groups, or audio-visual and conference specialists. The audio-visual specialists normally have all the facilities for producing complete programmes — designers, writers, photographers, sound recordists and special equipment such as rostrum cameras, programming consoles and increasingly, computer graphics terminals. Some of them employ full-time writers but many prefer to hire the most suitable writer for the project on a freelance basis.

You can get details of audio-visual production companies from directories like *Advertiser's Annual* or the *Creative Handbook. Campaign, Marketing* and *Audio Visual* magazines publish regular features on the market and suppliers, while the Association of Conference Executives publish an annual *Conference Services Directory* that lists producers and other suppliers.

Films and video

Despite the technical brilliance of slide projection, many people prefer the action of film and video. Film and video are used in similar applications to slides — training, presentation, education and information. The programmes are produced in-house, or by specialist companies and independent producers. Any of these organisations or individuals could be in the market for scripts, so it is important to keep in touch and to understand the application and requirements of the media.

Sponsored films

Film has two main roles — training or information; commissioned films are used only by the company that buys them, while sponsored films are made for company use but may be released for public viewing. Some of the best sponsored films have become classics in their own right. The GPO film unit's *Night Mail* is perhaps the most famous.

Many companies use film to explain their policies and attitudes to the public. Often these films have an additional, important, educational function. The Shell Film Unit, for example, produces a whole range of first-class films on topics that are related to oil, including weather, geology, fishing and exploration. Because of the large budgets involved, most of this work comes from larger organisations such as the oil companies, the National Coal Board or the Electricity Council.

Instruction films

Instruction or training films are very tightly scripted because the producer is looking for definite results and feedback from the audience. Although creativity is important it should only be used to make explanation clearer, and not for its own sake.

Before filming begins all the shots are worked out in strict sequence, and the script is carefully tested to make sure that it is completely comprehensible. You need to be aware of the techniques that are available to the makers of instruction films — animation, graphics, stop-motion photography, archive film and library material.

Video

Video is the newest of the audio-visual media, and is used in broadcast and non-broadcast form. In the business and training sector it has made a strong impact, but it has not ousted film as some people had predicted. Video does not yet have the reproduction quality that is needed for large screen projection, so it is used primarily for viewing on a monitor, and for presentation to small groups. It does have distinct advantages over film where immediate access to material and instant reply are important. Film and video are now beginning to establish their separate identities and applications. Video is becoming more common as an in-house medium, and many large companies have formed their own production units to handle the growing demand for promotional and training material. They would primarily use staff writers, either because the programmes are on complex technical subjects, or because the budget does not allow for the cost of outside suppliers. However, there are companies that use outside writers for overload or for special projects. *Audio Visual* magazine publishes regular articles on companies that run their own video unit.

Video magazines are often used in employee relations, either to keep them up to date with developments, or to report particular topics like the annual financial results. These programmes are a mix of interviews, features, reports and graphic presentations — a mix that calls for versatility in the writer.

Companies who sell their products through retail outlets are beginning to use video as a display aid. In large do-it-yourself stores, for example, there is usually an area where customers can see programmes about particular projects or products. The programmes are sponsored by the manufacturer. Estate agents and travel agents use pre-recorded cassettes to show potential customers details of homes or holidays.

Video is also used in special training applications where role-playing and instant replay are important. It is also used in community broadcasting by the police, public bodies and local organisations as part of their community relations programme. Your research should cover public and local government, as well as industry.

Pre-recorded video

Pre-recorded video cassettes are being produced in increasing numbers to meet the very large training demand, and the growing needs of the domestic market. If you look at catalogues published by audio-visual hire companies, you can see the growth areas — management, training, health and safety at work, industrial relations, and retail development. *Audio visual* magazine regularly reviews new programmes.

In the domestic market much of the output is re-recording of existing material from film stock, with the biggest single area in successful movies. But there are specialised video publishing groups producing programmes on a wide variety of subjects — particularly sports and games. The technology is becoming increasingly sophisticated with developments in interactive video and video disc which give the programme producer even greater creative freedom. To succeed as a writer in this area, you need a good grasp of video technology.

Scripts for film and video

If you are commissioned to write a script for film or video you become part of a production team, and you are rarely called on to produce just a script. In any programme there are a number of preliminary stages.

First there is a planning meeting to discuss the objective of the programme and the target audience, and to establish the main theme, schedule and budget. You are usually given access to a group of contacts and available research material. After you have researched your material you produce a treatment; this is not a script, but an indication of your approach and the subject matter to be covered by the programme.

Only when this and the budget have been agreed can the script begin. Not all programmes can be completely scripted before shooting. Travel, wildlife or industrial export programmes are usually assembled and finally scripted before editing. An initial structure is important, but too tight a script would not allow for the unexpected.

Final scripts should contain all the instructions for shooting, sound and visual effects; you need to work closely with the producer to achieve this. If you are not familiar with the particular problems of setting out script and visual treatment you can take one of the correspendence courses that cover the subject.

Film and video projects progress in clearly defined stages and may occupy a considerable period of time. It is important to establish a feasible timetable that you can meet and that will allow you to meet other commitments. It is also important to negotiate stage payments so that you are paid as you complete each section. If the project stops for any reason you are then assured of payment for work you have already completed.

Chapter 7
Poetry and Stage Plays

The market for published poetry is extremely small. Outside the education sector there are few volumes of poetry published, even by leading poets. This is one of the few areas where private publishing is recommended as an alternative; in fact it may be the only resort.

Poetry magazines

Poetry's major outlet is the small number of specialised magazines that are published with a subsidy from the Arts Council — magazines like the *New Review*. The Poetry Society publish *Poetry Review* and there are independent magazines that publish poetry but are not subsidised. They pay minimal fees, if any, and some give only a free copy of the magazine.

There are still some general interest magazines that will accept poetry contributions, although the opportunities are few. The magazines that offer a market for verse include women's magazines that publish domestic verse; poetry of a regional flavour in local or county magazines and opportunities in the literary magazines and the Sundays.

Collections of poetry

The prospects for publishing collections of poetry are not great either. Where the poems are part of an anthology, the publisher pays a copyright fee for the use of previously published material. That fee is normally split between the author and original publisher. There are a small number of publishing houses that deal only with poetry, and publish on a shoestring. You can find details of them in *Writers' and Artists' Year Book*.

Self-publishing for poets

However, for many poets, the only choice is to organise their own publishing and sell copies directly to customers or to the retail trade. You pay a printer to produce the books for you and then take any profits from sales as your income.

Provided the book sells reasonably well you could earn some income, perhaps equivalent to a small royalty. If you use the subscription method you get a better indication of the potential sales level and your profit. Here, buyers agree to buy a copy of the book before publication. They usually get a discount on the published price and you get a guaranteed income that should at least cover your production costs.

Poetry on radio

Radio 3 produces two programmes on poetry — the 'Living Poet', an occasional programme that deals with the work of one poet only, and 'Poetry Now', a monthly programme lasting 20 minutes, in which poets read selections from their own work. You should write to the producer of 'Poetry Now' with examples of your work.

Stage plays

The distribution and market for stage plays are very different from film; they have a number of separate local markets. Plays are not released on general distribution but the performance rights are sold for use in different theatres. So a play might be licensed for production in, say, the Chelmsford Civic Theatre; it would earn a fee based on the length of the run, and also a percentage of the box office takings.

While most playwrights have the ambition to get a play produced in the West End or on Broadway, the usual starting place is in local theatre where fees are minimal. However, it helps the new writer to get established and there may be an opportunity to share in the profits if the production is successful.

If a play is very successful it may be taken up by West End theatre management and produced there. It could also go on a provincial tour with a repertory company, or be licensed to a nominated company to produce in local theatres. The income basis would be the same — the length of run and the income from box office receipts.

You can get details of plays that are in production or companies that are looking for plays in the magazine *Stage and Television Today*, or in the magazines of the regional Arts

Associations. *Writers' and Artists' Year Book* discusses the different types of licensing arrangement that apply at local, regional and West End level.

If you are writing for the stage you need to be aware of the mechanics of the theatre — how to get characters on and off the stage, how to cope with changes of scenery and costume and to write plays that are a suitable length for a full performance. Books or courses on stage management or amateur dramatics would be useful, or alternatively you could join a local dramatic society to get practical experience of this work.

Authors of plays can also earn a royalty income from the sale of published versions of their works. Faber and French are probably the leading publishers of this type of book.

Chapter 8

Writing for the Educational Market

Educational writing is not confined to ex-teachers or professional educators, though they are possibly the main providers. Teaching experience could be valuable to a writer who is preparing textbooks for a specific course, but communication skills are far more important.

There are many different opportunities in educational writing — in books, films, audio-visual material, radio and television. Some of the biggest selling books in the world are textbooks. Schools broadcasting remains an important part of the output of radio and television, and there are new opportunities with the continuing growth of adult education.

Despite educational cutbacks, there is still a substantial demand for course material. With the introduction of new technology into schools — video, computers, interactive video discs and teaching machines for example — much of the traditional teaching material will need to be adapted for new media. What will not change is the high standards of writing required.

Educational standards

Publishers in this market have a responsibility to children and teachers to ensure that books and programmes meet general educational and curriculum requirements. In many cases they retain an educational consultant to advise on the content of material that is in preparation. The consultants may lay down strict guidelines on content and the language to be used. These form part of the brief to the author and ensure consistency. In television and radio the Schools Broadcasting Council carry out the same role. The educational writer works within strict disciplines.

Know the syllabus

Educational writing must be specific to a particular age group and course. The main divisions are into primary, secondary and tertiary sections, with a growing level of activity in adult education. Within those broad areas are very wide differences in age and ability. The writer needs to understand the courses that the different age groups are taking. You can get information on the courses from local authorities, examination bodies and teachers' centres.

In the further education sector the picture becomes more complicated, with a bewildering array of college and university courses. There are full- and part-time courses and they lead to a wide range of academic, vocational and professional qualifications. You can get details of courses from career or further education guides in libraries or career centres. Information on syllabuses may be obtainable from the same sources, or directly from colleges and universities. Another statistic that can help you indicate the potential of your book is the number of candidates who enter for specific exams. You can get information on previous years' figures from the various examining bodies.

The important point is that the more you know about a course, the more tightly targeted your work will be, and the greater the chance of its acceptance. This can be very difficult for someone without teaching experience. Textbooks must be written carefully to relate to course content and the text must be practical. Outsiders are at a relative disadvantage. There is also the problem of course changes. New courses mean new editions, but you have to be aware of the changes to recognise the opportunity.

Team writing

Another aspect of the education market is the high incidence of team writing. Here a group of writers contribute their own particular skills or areas of knowledge to a book or project. They may form a group to offer their own proposals to a publisher, or they may be brought together by sponsors to tackle more complex projects. The sponsors could be a public body, local authority or publisher. In a multi-media project, for example, you might find an editor, several authors, consultants, illustrators, translators and researchers. Not all the team would be employed full time, nor would they all take an equal share of the fee or royalties for the project.

Books

Despite the inroads made by new technology, books continue to dominate. You should contact publishers who have a strong educational activity, companies like Longman or Macmillan, for example, or specialist children's publishing companies like Ladybird. Before you send your proposal, check to see which educational sectors they are involved in — primary, secondary or higher education (tertiary).

Book fairs and educational conferences give you the opportunity to meet publishers' representatives, and to get their assessment of the types of books that are selling, and the books that are needed. Your research should include school libraries and publishers' catalogues. A number of organisations can offer useful advice on existing material and book requirements; they include the National Textbook Reference Library, School Library Association, Council for Subject Teaching Association and School Government Publishing Company.

An educational textbook is likely to be assessed very critically before publication, so a more detailed proposal will be needed. In the initial proposal you need to put forward the reasons why your book is suitable for the course, explaining how it follows the syllabus, and demonstrating why your version introduces more effective material than any other book. The synopsis should relate content to the course, and your sample chapter should indicate your ability to explain difficult concepts. You also need to indicate the sort of illustrative material that will support and clarify the text. Your publisher will expect you to have a strong grasp of the subject matter, but you can substantiate this by stating your qualifications for writing the book: subject expertise or relevant teaching experience, for example.

If you are writing a book that forms part of an existing series, you will be working to tight editorial guidelines. In a long-running or wide-ranging series, the books will probably be written to established publishing schedules. There would also be strict target dates where books are prepared for a new syllabus. Timing can be critical in educational books.

You also have to build in an allowance for validation of a textbook. Before a textbook is printed and published it has to be validated in a classroom. Once again teaching experience can prove valuable, both in anticipating problems and providing the right contacts among people who could validate the book for you, although the publisher could probably help.

A most useful little book for educational writers is *Publishing for Schools* (Educational Publishers Council, 19 Bedford Square, London WC1B 3HJ; 01-580 6321).

Audio visual

Audio-visual aids are now an important part of educational resources. Most schools and colleges are equipped with 'learning centres' or 'resource centres'. These are either self-contained units where projection equipment is permanently installed, or storage areas where equipment and programmes are borrowed and used in other classrooms.

The centres keep or hire hardware or programmes to support the subjects in the curriculum. Where the material is needed for a long time, it is usually bought outright, but if it is needed only for short or single sessions, it would normally be hired, either direct from the sponsor or maker of the programme, or from a specialised hire operator like Guild Sound and Vision. The resources would probably be a mix of films, filmstrips, slide-tape programmes, overhead projector transparencies, and perhaps video cassettes.

Writing for audio visual is discussed in Chapter 6, but the requirements of educational A/V are very different from those of commercial programmes. As with books, the content and text must be of a very high standard, and will be closely monitored by educational experts. Educational programmes will be published for general use as course material rather than just made for a specific conference or presentation.

To meet the demand, some publishing companies in the education market run separate audio-visual divisions. Longman, for example, have an education division which has its own audio-visual unit producing a range of material for schools and colleges. There are a number of production companies who believe that the future of educational publishing is in audio visual; they are developing a broad range of programmes for all educational levels. Companies too can supply educational programmes. Of the oil companies, Shell and BP have a very active education department and their film units have won numerous awards.

To find out who is making or sponsoring programmes, you should study hire catalogues and then contact the makers directly to ask about script-writing opportunities. You can also do field research at local resource centres.

Study aids

It's not just textbooks and programmes that are required for a course; there is a whole range of study aids and back-up material to help students. The Kogan Page book *Producing Teaching Materials* by Henry Ellington gives much valuable advice to a writer working in this field. Study aids and back-up material should be written and produced to the same high standards as the main material. To support textbooks there are handbooks or manuals for the teacher, original documents, special research papers, collections of relevant articles, and digest reprints of other material. The amount of original writing is small; rather it is a process of editing existing material, but the editing needs to be carefully structured to provide useful support material.

Audio-visual publishers who supply programmes also produce a full range of back-up material. This would include copies of the script, guidelines for the teacher, question and answer sheets, work-books based on the programme, and study aids such as wallcharts. The aim is to produce a complete package so that the audio-visual programme is an integrated part of the syllabus.

The writer is concerned with more than just a text, he is producing an educational kit. This type of project requires co-operation with many other people — designers, photographers, audio-visual technicians — and sometimes specialised companies outside the educational market will be set up to produce them.

Schools broadcasting

Schools broadcasting is an established part of the educational system. The programmes are not part of a curriculum, but an additional resource for the teacher. Programmes are broadcast morning and afternoon throughout the school year and have to be carefully scheduled to suit the curriculum.

That means the writer will be working well in advance of broadcasting dates. A whole year's programmes have to be ready for broadcast six months in advance. If you add production lead times to that, then scripts or ideas should be in a producer's hands at least 18 months before a planned broadcasting date.

In the BBC, education programmes on radio and television are handled jointly by one controller and there are four types of output — schools (television and radio) and continuing education (radio and television). Many programmes are written by producers or staff writers, although they do use outside writers and welcome ideas for new programmes. Producers also retain education consultants to advise them on content and course requirement. The Schools Broadcasting Council consisting mainly of educationists, acts in an overall advisory capacity on programme standards.

Continuing education

Continuing education programmes cover a wide range of topics including work, leisure, arts, science, recreation, literacy, technology and languages. Programme planning is on a similar time-scale to schools broadcasting and is also published in the pamphlet, 'Annual Programmes'.

The major breakthrough in continuing education was the establishment of the Open University. It has not, however, provided any significant opportunities for freelance writers. The BBC provides broadcasting services for the OU and there are books and support material to accompany the courses.

The Open University offers traditional university courses, but there are no resident students. 'Lectures' are broadcast on television and students send in assignments by post. The courses cover the whole spectrum of university education and are outlined in a prospectus available from the Registrar, The Open University, Walton Hall, Milton Keynes MK7 6AA; 0908 84066. Course directors and tutors are the equivalent of university lecturers. They produce their own course material and are helped in this by the central design and broadcasting resources of the OU. Most programmes are scripted by BBC producers in conjunction with Open University academics but there are opportunities for writers to put forward proposals for new series or proposals on special subjects. They should include details of their qualifications and areas of interest.

Chapter 9
Business Publications

Providing editorial services to companies is a distinct branch of freelance writing. Here the writer does not choose his topic or work on commission, but acts on a specific brief from a business client or agency to provide writing services. This can be for *ad hoc* projects or it may be a regular service.

Work for companies falls into a number of different categories. The most common is publicity work which can take many forms. Companies have to provide information to their shareholders and customers. This may be a legal requirement, as in the case of annual reports, or it may be to support their marketing programmes through the provision of promotional material. Many industrial products need instruction material, and companies may carry out public relations programmes aimed either at their own employees or at groups of people who are likely to have an interest in the company's activities.

Staff or freelance writers?

All of these documents require text, though much of it is written by people within the company. However, companies do retain writers, either through advertising agencies and public relations consultancies, or on an editoral fee basis. Traditionally, companies have used outside writers for creative advertising copywriting or for the preparation of press releases, but an increasing number are realising the value of using an editorial consultancy to write or edit other forms of company literature.

Company reports

Take the company annual report as an example. Once the mere tabulation of figures, relieved only by the chairman's review, it now incorporates an illustrated section reviewing the company's principal activities and indicating its strengths and recent performances.

The skill of the writer is to prepare text that will help the stockbroker, banker, investment analyst or shareholder to assess the performance of the company they are investing in, and to decide whether that company's prospects are worth pursuing. The topics the writer is likely to cover include company organisation, growth, sales and export record, labour relations, principal customers, and prospects in their markets. To write about these assumes a certain level of knowledge of the company's activities and also a degree of access to the board of the company. Annual reports are normally handled by the company secretary or a board member, and their preparation is surrounded by a considerable degree of security — security that is obviously in the company's interest, but is also a requirement of the Stock Exchange.

Employee communications

Many companies produce annual reports for their employees. These are written in a much lighter style, and their intention is to explain to employees how the company is performing, and encourage them to make their own contribution to the company's progress. It takes considerable writing skills to interpret complicated company activities, and to present statistics so that they are meaningful and understandable. This calls for an ability to communicate information clearly.

The employee annual report is just one aspect of what is known as employee communications. Company newspapers are another medium. In large organisations they are produced quarterly, or sometimes more frequently. The story content is mixed, containing news of successful sales, new appointments, business opportunities, changes in organisation, developments in manufacturing or administration, and sports and social news. The aim is to tell people what is going on in their part of the company, and to keep them informed of developments that might affect them.

The main problem about producing this kind of newspaper is getting the raw material for the stories. If the writer is not a member of the company he or she depends on input from other people, and this sort of information is not always forthcoming. An alternative is for the writer to take on the role of reporter and gather the material personally. To be successful you need to establish good contacts within many different departments and keep in touch regularly.

Preparing and handling copy for a newspaper can be time-consuming. Initially the company establishes a list of contents, determined by the story material available and also by the requirements of various departments such as marketing and personnel. Next comes the reporting stage, and then draft stories are prepared for approval. There may be several rewrites for content or length before the newspaper finally goes to press. You should always build in allowances for change when you estimate your fee for producing newspaper copy.

Companies also produce newspapers for customers and sales prospects. The content is a mixture of product successes, manufacturing developments, new products, and other topics that affect customer service. The aim is to indicate this efficiency of the company as a supplier. You may get the opportunity to prepare all the copy, by reporting and writing, or you may contribute articles or news items to the editor.

Technical publications

Companies who manufacture products for the industrial market — electrical equipment, engineering components, heavy machinery, for example — produce a large number of technical publications including catalogues, sales leaflets, design manuals and instruction material. They are used by engineers in the customers company to evaluate a technical product, and the publications form an important part of the selling process. The information for technical publications would be collated by someone within a company because it requires a high level of detailed product knowledge. The writer would probably be given a rough text to edit or rewrite. The problem for the writer is to make the text comprehensible without making it simplistic. Here you are not writing for the layman, but for an expert who understands the technology and is assessing the supplier's technical competence.

Training and instruction material is often written by people within the company, though that is not always an advantage. A criticism aimed at engineers who produce this type of material is that they are really too familiar with the subject; their explanations or instructions can take too much for granted. Writers who are new to the product have to understand it themselves, and put themselves in the position of the reader. Instruction material can vary from a single sheet to a series of complicated and detailed manuals on a sophisticated product. The aim is always clarity.

Computer manuals

With the advent of the electronic office, many companies are having to carry out a major training exercise to familiarise staff with new technology and, in many cases, to instruct them in its use. This is work that could be carried out by the company or by the suppliers of the equipment. Computer documentation is a growing area for the writer, but not necessarily for the writer who knows about computers. In the second generation of computer sales, the users are not data processing people who require complex operating manuals that enable them to achieve sophisticated results, but clerical and managerial staff who, in computer terms, are 'unskilled'.

What they need are instruction manuals that enable them to carry out their daily tasks easily. Ease of use is a major selling platform of modern computing systems, and simple document-ation is what everyone in the industry is looking for. The data processing department feel the same way; they are faced with an overwhelming demand from business users for training and support. The rapid growth of the home computing market has shown people how simple computing can be, but there is still a substantial training task. Documentation plays a vital part.

Customers for computer documentation would include computer manufacturers — the people who make the hardware; software houses — they make programs to run on other people's hardware; and computer users — the companies with large computer installations, and many new users. Your contacts within the companies could be in the personnel, training or data processing departments. You can get information on the companies who are using computers by reading the business computing trade press. They run stories on company appli-cations and new installations.

The main requirement is clear, simple user manuals that will allow a new user to begin computing easily and quickly, without leaving the office for long courses. At present, manuals are large, imposing documents which tend to frighten off potential users. The aim is simplicity, and a number of progressive companies would be pleased to reduce basic instructions to fit on a postcard. Ideally the user would be able to sit down at a keyboard and operate the system in a matter of hours.

In the past, instruction manuals have been written by the engineer who developed the system. Now they ask a writer to edit the text for clarity. The best way to do this is to sit down with a keyboard and program and write your instructions as you use the system. If you are unfamiliar with the system you will be approaching it as a new user, and you should be able to describe operations in the simplest possible way.

Writing with designers

Business publications move through a spectrum from factual documents to promotional publications. At the promotional end of the spectrum the visual element becomes more important and writers need to work closely with designers. Corporate brochures, sales leaflets, direct mail shots and press advertisements — these are all areas where visual and text support each other to create a selling message.

In advertising agencies a creative team works on a client's account to produce press advertisements and television commercials. The same team would be together for a considerable period of time so that they gain experience of the client's products and markets.

You don't need that sort of formal relationship to produce other business publications, but you do need to be in contact with a designer to establish that text length is suitable and to discuss the ways in which photographs or illustrations strengthen the message.

Who buys writing services?

The writer's main point of contact within a company is likely to be the people responsible for publicity. They go under a vareity of names including publicity manager, public relations manager, advertising manager, head of communications, marketing services manager and sales promotion manager. They may have a small staff that could include writers and designers but is more likely to consist of other administrators. They deal with outside suppliers, briefing them, checking work and monitoring costs against publicity budgets.

They, in turn, have clients within their own company who need writing or design services, but who do not have the expertise to deal directly with specialist suppliers. The publicity manager acts as the link, even though the ultimate customer may be someone like the technical manager, the director of marketing, or the head of personnel.

In a case like that you could be briefed by the publicity manager on behalf of his client. This has advantages and drawbacks.

The advantage is that you get a professional brief and professional comments on your work, but the drawback is that you may not get the whole story, but only one person's interpretation of it. When you come to present your text you could be criticised for inadequate content, a situation that is clearly not your fault. A far more satisfactory arrangement is to meet both publicity manager and client, and to have access to the client for further information.

A similar complication could occur if you are referred to the company's advertising agency or public relations consultancy. This situation could arise when the publicity manager acts purely as an administrator and has all the work produced by the agency or consultancy. They would be given a budget to cover publicity activities, and they become your customer.

Agencies and consultancies employ full-time writers but they are primarily used to prepare advertisements and press releases. Advertising agencies sometimes have to buy in special writing and design skills for projects like brochures, annual reports or other publications that they handle for their clients as part of a total service.

Public relations consultancies also handle special projects for their clients. They supply information for the press or for corporate and financial relations. Press releases are used to send regular items of news to the media; they would normally be handled within the consultancy because confidentiality and speed are critical. However, some of their work is suitable for the freelance writer. They produce feature articles for the trade press that are attributed to members of the company and are often highly technical. These articles help to improve the company's image as a technically competent supplier. The company would normally give a detailed brief on content and would check text before it goes for publication.

Selling writing services

However, when you are offering writing services to a company your initial approach should be to the publicity manager. If writing is not his responsibility, he will put you in touch with the right person. You can get the names of company publicity staff from publications such as the *Advertiser's Annual* or the *BRAD Advertiser and Agency List*. These books catalogue the companies that have an active publicity operation, describe their main products and name the people responsible for publicity. The most important trade magazines for the publicity industry are *Campaign* and *Marketing*. They give news of the companies who are currently running advertising campaigns, changes in accounts and appointments within the industry. Their recruitment advertisements often give clues to the structure of internal publicity departments and the ways in which they use outside suppliers.

When you make contact you may get an opportunity to present your work. The customer will assess you on your experience of writing publicity material and your knowledge of his particular products and markets. The more relevant your experience, the greater are your chances of meeting his requirements. Ideally you should have examples of relevant work to back up your claims. Designers, for example, when they are presenting for that type of work, use a portfolio to show samples of printed work.

Briefs and approvals

If you are successful you may be asked to put forward proposals for a future project. You would be briefed on the aims of the project, provided with background and detail information, and given a timetable for proposals, draft text and final copy. If you work for a well-organised company you may be asked to submit a briefing document. Here you summarise the brief to show that you have interpreted it correctly. You outline the objectives your copy is to meet, the audience you are writing for, and the main copy points to be brought out.

On an *ad hoc* project like this you would be paid a fee for supplying final copy and your estimate should take account of the various intermediate stages. One of the difficulties about charging for business copywriting is costing changes. Where the customer introduces new information then this is clearly an author's correction, and the additional work should be charged. Where you are asked to change copy because the customer feels it is wrong, the position is more difficult. You may feel you have been wrongly briefed, or the client is changing his mind, in which case you should stand firm and charge for the additional work. If the responsibility is less clear-cut, it may be difficult to put in extra charges. A written briefing document can help you avoid that situation.

Costing writing services

There are two ways to cost an *ad hoc* project. You can put in an estimated price for the whole job based on your assessment of the time to complete, or you can simply quote an hourly rate with a reasonable forecast of the total time. The hourly rate is more suitable for long projects where you cannot predict your total involvement. The fixed price estimate is usually only practical where the project is clear-cut and you can rely on your customer to be straightforward in his dealings with you.

If your work is successful and you get the opportunity of regular writing assignments there is an alternative method of costing. Instead of a price per project you quote a fee for providing writing services. This could be a monthly or an annual figure and your obligation is to meet the customer's requirements within that figure. This method has the advantage of giving you a more stable form of income, but the onus is on you to get your costings right. Where the customer has a definite programme of projects the method can work, but if your customer is vague, and only plans in the short term, you could find yourself heavily committed for a poor return.

Working for agencies and consultancies

You also have the opportunity to work for advertising agencies and public relations consultancies directly. The problem of minimal contact with the ultimate client is still there, but in this case the agency is your client, and not the customer company. It is their responsibility to brief you accurately. The payment structure is similar: you can either be paid *ad hoc* fees or given a retainer to provide writing services.

There are a number of problems in working indirectly through an agency. Your work is likely to be anonymous if you are used as a freelance writer. It is the agency that is credited with the work, not you. If you are named as the writer then you might get a reputation as an expensive writer through no fault of your own. The agency has to make a profit so they would add a handling charge to the figure that you invoice them. The final problem is instability. If you make a commitment to one agency, and do little sales development of your own, your prospects are tied to theirs. If they begin to lose business you could find yourself with a short-term problem.

Chapter 10
Writing Services

Writing services cover a wide range of research, teaching and writing activities that publishers and other writers use to supplement their own resources. The scope of the activities includes research, teaching, indexing, proof-reading, rewriting, editing, book packaging and syndication.

Magazine editorial services

Editorial and design consultancies handle the preparation of copy and make-up for entire magazines or specific sections. Here they write or commission articles, select photographs or illustrations, do page layouts and hand over a number of pages ready for production. This could cover a specific topic such as holidays or gardening, or embrace a special features section whose content and topics vary from issue to issue. This frees staff writers and designers to concentrate on the rest of the publication. However, the magazine editor and art editor would maintain close liaison to control style and content and make sure that the material conforms to the rest of the magazine.

This type of service is particularly valuable to a new periodical that has not yet recruited staff writers, and which needs to establish an editorial format. The brief would be to prepare a format for a magazine aimed at a particular audience, together with a production budget, print specification and statement of editorial policy.

You can find out about plans for new magazines in *Campaign*, and in the recruitment pages of *Campaign* or the *Guardian* on Monday, under Creative and Media Appointments. These advertisements announce opportunities for a large number of staff to run a new magazine.

Book packaging

Books or series of books can be put together in a similar way. Where publishers have an idea for a series of books, they may undertake the packaging work themselves or they may use an editorial consultancy to put together a package. It might be format only, or comprehensive, covering the entire process up to production stage.

From the publisher's initial brief for a book, or a series of books on a specific topic, aimed at a particular audience, you would prepare an outline of content and format of the book in terms of number of pages, and extent of illustrations for initial approval. You would then either write the text or commission other authors to do this, taking editorial responsibility for their work. To complete the book you can carry out picture research and supply photographs and illustrations, preparing a layout and type mark-up of the text for the publisher. The book is then ready for final editing and production.

To offer the comprehensive service you need to cooperate with designers and picture researchers unless you have these skills yourself and, for a large project, you would be working with other writers and editors. There is no obvious way to research this area. To find out about opportunities you need to keep in constant touch with publishers.

Syndication

Syndication is a method of selling the same article or photograph to a number of different publications in the UK and overseas. Suitable material would include cartoons, comic strips, or articles on topics such as motoring, medical, gardening, holidays or other subjects with a universal appeal.

Sometimes a single article of outstanding quality can be syndicated, but a series of articles appearing at weekly or monthly intervals is more suitable. The editor relies on a guaranteed regular feature so you have to be able to deliver on time, sometimes weeks in advance. You get paid a fee for each insertion so the way to build the business is to increase the number of outlets for your work.

Translation services

If you speak foreign languages, translation can be a useful source of work. For fiction books you should contact publishers directly with details of your experience and samples of your translated work. In addition to a translation fee you may also be able to negotiate a royalty on sales of the translated edition.

Non-fiction work can have two sources, either direct from the publisher or through a translation agency. If you are translating non-fiction material, particularly technical subjects, you need to know the technical terms that are used. Literal translations don't always work. Translation agencies have full-time translators for the principal languages they cover, but they use freelance translators for other languages and for technical subjects that require expert knowledge.

It needn't just be translations from foreign languages. There are an increasing number of books from Canada, the USA or other English-speaking countries that are relevant to the UK market, but need modification to be acceptable or to conform to UK practice. Educational or business handbooks, for example, may need to be rewritten to meet the requirements of a British syllabus or to reflect British business practice. Where a marketing book uses case studies as an integral part of the presentation, many of these may be irrelevant; they need to be based on British marketing and purchasing organisations, selling practices, legal restrictions and ethics. Apart from that there are the more obvious editorial changes to spelling, units of measurement and geographical references.

Publishers treat this as an editing exercise rather than a rewrite and they normally pay an outright fee for the service. Although any publisher is likely to handle a number of 'imported English' books you should concentrate your sales effort on the multinational publishers who have a UK office, or on publishers who state that they specialise in books of this type.

Research services

Publishers, broadcasting companies and other writers use researchers on a contract or freelance basis. You can either research a subject in which you have expert knowledge, or you can be a general researcher with the ability to track down difficult sources, published references, and locate contacts for a variety of subjects.

In the *Guardian* Creative and Media Appointments section, published on Mondays, there are advertisements for different types of researcher. Television companies, for example, look for a researcher to work on a historical series, a radio company needs one to conduct interviews and gather material for a consumer affairs programme, an independent television production company seeks an expert researcher to contribute to a wildlife programme. *Radio Times* and *TV Times* name reseachers in programme credits, but these may be researchers on long-term contract to the television company.

Picture research is a specialist service for the publisher, writer or producer who is working on illustrated books or television programmes. Publishers who use freelance picture researchers often issue contracts for each assignment. The picture researcher either suggests the types of illustrations that would be suitable or locates subjects specified by the publishers or author. There are a number of sources for these — special picture libraries, photo agencies, newspapers, libraries, museums and private collections. Many of them publish a catalogue or index of the subjects they hold and the researcher needs to have up-to-date reference material. Useful directories include *Picture Researcher's Handbook* (Saturday Ventures) ed Hilary Evans, *Sources of Illustration 1500-1900* (Adams and Dart), and *Directory of British Photographic Collections* (Heinemann).

If you are handling photographs you will become involved in administration. Some libraries and museums make search fees for locating material. You also have to pay reproduction fees, copyright fees and cost of producing copies or prints. You have to obtain copyright clearance and the right to reproduce, as well as acknowledging the sources, writing captions and making sure that the material is safely returned after publication.

Ghost writing

There are opportunities as a ghost writer, rewriting manuscripts that in their original state are virtually unpublishable, or originating books, working with famous people and writing a text that eventually appears under the subject's name. These could include memoirs of a famous personality, sports biographies, or other texts that show promise but are totally lacking in any sort of writing quality. This is another area where the writer has to suffer anonymity because he or she is acting only as editor. You would get an undigested manuscript with a brief to turn it into something readable that is a more manageable length for publication.

Editing, indexing, proof-reading

These are general editorial services that you can offer to

publishers. They use freelance services either to supplement their own resources when there is a heavy workload, or to get specialist help on a particular topic where expert knowledge is essential. The Society of Indexers is involved with the Rapid Results College in running a correspondence course on methods of indexing. They also maintain a register of qualified indexers which they circulate free to publishers to get work for members.

Teaching writing

Teaching represents a potentially valuable source of income for the experienced writer. While many people in arts and crafts teach to supplement their freelance income, relatively few writers have explored this area. Teaching can take a number of forms; providing teaching services to established teaching or training organisations; or developing your own courses and teaching individually.

Teaching on a writing course
Many local authorities, for example, run adult education classes in creative writing; the course tutors are established authors who are able to give students the benefit of their professional experience. They may teach students a set syllabus, but their main contribution is the inspiration and professional criticism they bring to students' work. The courses are held during term time, often in the evening, so you need to be available whenever the course is running.

Those are regular teaching positions. Occasional courses are run by a number of private organisations. The Writing School and the Arvon Foundation are examples of two specialist teaching groups who provide residential and occasional day courses for writers throughout the year. The courses are a combination of lecture and workshop session in which students work under supervision. Although groups like this employ their own permanent teaching staff, they also use specialist writers to teach specific topics beyond their own expertise.

Training groups offering courses in management and communications skills to business are increasingly including writing courses in their prospectuses. The writing functions are different — reports, correspondence and other forms of business writing — but they still depend on the teaching of basic writing skills. These business courses are held either on a company's premises — internal courses for one company only — or at hotels, where the courses are open to any delegates.

Payment for organised courses like these is a combination of fees and expenses. Delegates and students pay the organiser a specified fee, and the organiser pays you for your contribution. You would also receive expenses to cover the cost of travel between your home and the course venue. If the course is residential and you need to stay overnight or longer, the costs of your accommodation and meals would normally be covered by the organiser. The fee covers your presence at the course as a teacher or presenter; you need to discuss with the organiser whether it also covers the cost of any teaching materials such as duplicated notes, exercises, examples, and other reference materials. If their cost is substantial, this could reduce the value of your fee so you need to establish who pays for them.

To find out about opportunities on teaching courses, contact the organisers and tell them about your interests and areas of knowledge; if you have teaching experience, so much the better. If, on the other hand, your work is well known, you may be invited to take part by the organisers. You may, for example, be an expert or the only published writer on a specific writing technique, so your work has given you a degree of authority. There is no single source of information on writing courses, so you need to check the writing magazines (listed on page 136) for advertisements. Local adult education courses are run by local education authorities or other providers recognised by the Department of Education and Science, such as the Workers' Educational Association.

Before accepting you as a teacher or a presenter, the organisers may ask you for an outline or detailed proposal of the contents of your session. The techniques for preparing outlines are similar to those described on page 139 for book outlines. Alternatively, you may be asked to teach within an existing course; in that case, the organisers will send you a course syllabus to help you prepare your contribution.

Running your own writing course

As well as organised writing courses, there are opportunities for you to teach or lecture independently. You could teach local writers who want to learn basic writing skills or improve their writing. Special interest groups, such as local history societies or archaeological societies, are possible candidates for writing workshops; they write reports, articles and books and could benefit from improving their skills. To locate students, you can advertise your services in the local newspaper or put up notices in the library or local adult education centre.

If you have specific skills in business writing, you can offer your teaching skills to companies. An increasing number of communications companies — advertising agencies and public relations consultancies — recognise the importance of improving writing skills, and are running internal training courses for experienced staff and recent recruits. Public relations consultancies, for example, employ executives who combine the skills of account management and writing; their writing responsibilities include press releases, feature articles, presentations and brochure copy, and they often need to improve writing skills in those areas.

Locating prospects is more difficult here; companies who run internal training courses do not advertise the fact, although you can sometimes find reports in the appropriate trade press. The section on business writing describes methods of locating and contacting prospects in business. You should approach either the managing director or the training manager in larger companies.

To run your own writing courses, you do not need special premises; in most cases you will be teaching on location in someone's home, at a society's meeting place, or at a company's office. Teaching writing does not require special facilities — seating and a surface for the students to work on — and, unless you are working with large groups, you will not need projection or public address facilities. You will have to supply your own teaching materials and documentation, and the cost of this will have to be built into your charge for the course. The other part of the charge is for your time in running the course. The simplest way to calculate this is to decide on an hourly rate and multiply this by the length of the course and the number of delegates.

Teaching represents an additional source of regular income for the writer, in contrast to the fluctuating income from freelance writing, but it does require a regular commitment of time. Teaching should not be regarded as an easy option; it takes a particular skill to get the best from other people — an ability to analyse the process of writing and to be able to relate your own skills to a student's writing abilities or problems.

Writers in Residence

Already established in America, the Writer in Residence is becoming a more common figure in the UK. Writers in Residence are found in universities and colleges, arts centres and similar establishments. Under the scheme, the writer is paid a salary for a period of, say, a year, for carrying out a specified amount of teaching, and being available for consultation and certain functions. The position of Writer in Residence can give you the opportunity to work on a large project without financial problems, but you have to establish how much time you will be expected to commit to the position and how much time will be available for your own work. Vacancies are advertised in the media and education section of newspapers like the *Guardian*, or in arts or writing magazines.

Lecturing on your writing

Lecturing on your work is related to teaching. Here, your audience does not expect to be taught, but wants to be informed or entertained. In many ways the opportunities and contacts are similar — local societies, special interest groups and writers' courses invite writers to talk about their books, or about writing in general. They may be interested either in what you have written about or how you have written it.

You would be invited to talk for a period of say 30 minutes or an hour and to answer questions afterwards. The organisers pay fees and travelling expenses, although the fees for talking to local groups are often negligible. Lectures do, however, give you an opportunity to promote or sell copies of your book, and this in itself can prove valuable. Many observers believe that novelist Jeffrey Archer initially sold so well because he was a very popular speaker and used the opportunity to promote his books.

Conference speaking and contributions

Conferences provide another opportunity for the writer who is a specialist in one particular field. Conference organisers put on programmes of events throughout the year; each conference is aimed at a particular target audience and would be held on a single day or for a longer period. The normal format of the conference is four or five speakers per day talking for approximately 45 minutes each and answering questions afterwards.

The conference is built around a theme and the speakers are experts — including authors — or experienced professionals who contribute on different aspects of the conference theme.

There are two opportunities for the writer — to appear as a conference speaker and earn a speaker's fee, or to help the organisers develop the conference theme and programme. For the development fee, you prepare an outline of the conference, nominating the speakers and giving them a brief to work to. You would also be responsible for writing the text for the spring and autumn catalogues, the individual prospectus which is mailed to prospective delegates, and the conference programme.

The Association of Conference Executives publish an annual guide to conference facilities together with a bi-monthly magazine giving news of events. Conference programmes are often found as loose inserts in the business magazines of the target market, or as advertisements in management magazines. You can use the event information to develop a contact list of organisers running conferences in your field of experience.

Chapter 11

Presenting Work

If you put the manuscripts of a book, a television script, a magazine article and a publicity brochure side by side, you would notice a considerable difference in appearance. Yet, they all follow conventions that help translate your ideas into a finished product.

The manuscript is not just a record of the writer's thoughts. It is a working document that other people use to make their contribution to the production process. Editors make their comments on your text; typesetters turn it into a typescript; company publicity staff decide to spend large amounts of money on the copy that you supply; and cameramen, actors and directors use your script to create a film or television programme.

So, unless you provide a manuscript that is accurate and easy to follow, any errors or lack of clarity will only be compounded by other people. To avoid this, there are a number of guidelines that have evolved from practical experience. They don't tell you how to avoid grammatical or spelling mistakes, but they do tell you how to present information so that other people follow your intentions. They tell you the best way to submit manuscripts, and they are guidelines that apply, whatever form your words finally take.

Every manuscript you submit must be typed. Hand-written material is out. Although standards of typing vary, the characters are immediately recognisable. This is important because the people who handle your manuscript at a later stage will be working quickly, often under pressure, and the risk of error is high.

The convention of laying out a manuscript with generous margins and double spacing is universal. A layout like this has a number of benefits. It helps the person reading your manuscript to follow the material easily. The space between the lines allows you or the reader to make corrections legibly. The margins are for instructions or comments. They also enable the manuscript sheets to be gripped by a typesetter's clip without obscuring text. Marginal notes might act merely as a reminder to the reader to query a point or take some other action, but they could be more specific — typesetting instructions on printed material, or camera directions on a film or television script.

You may also need to supply more than one copy of the manuscript. The quantity depends on what the text is being used for, but you should always keep one copy for yourself. If anything should go wrong while your only copies are in transit, or in somebody else's hands, you could lose a lot of money. The catalogue of possible disasters is endless — manuscripts lost in the post, damaged by coffee, sent to the wrong address, misfiled and never retrieved. That doesn't imply that the people who handle manuscripts are incompetent or careless, it just means they can make mistakes. It is your responsibility to keep one permanent record of your own work. This is important even if you prepare your manuscripts electronically on a word processor for example, and submit a disc. Discs run the same risks of loss or damage, so copy the material on to a back-up disc, or print out the text and keep the paper copy as a record.

Preliminary proposals can save you money

Not every piece of paper you send to a publisher or producer will be a final manuscript. In many cases it saves time and money to submit a preliminary letter or synopsis before starting a project (see page 16).

This preliminary material should be prepared to the same standards as the manuscript, but it needs the essential ingredient of selling power. The aim of the letter or synopsis is to persuade the reader to commission a piece of work from you — an article, book, script or screenplay. The readers are already looking for this type of material; their decision to buy your proposal depends on many factors, and your preliminary material should supply the right information.

Who is the book or programme aimed at? Is that their audience? How much will it cost to produce? Is the budget available? How does it compare with existing material? Does it break new ground, or is it similar to something that has been recently published? The quality of your work is judged later; at this stage the reader needs to be convinced that it fits the market.

What you include in the proposal depends on the medium

you are writing for, but it is useful to have a general checklist of information that your reader is likely to need. In book publishing a number of companies ask prospective authors to complete a form that covers this ground. If you use a checklist you can be sure of including all the information you need, and the information will be in a form that is ready to use. This is useful to the people who read your proposal because they, in turn, will have to sell the proposal to someone else.

Your checklist should certainly include the aims and main audience for the work; the length, in number of words or running time; the reasons why the work breaks new ground; what stage the project has reached so far, and the anticipated completion date; the number of photographs or illustrations you plan to include in a printed work; in film or television, the number of characters, locations and props; your qualifications for writing the work and your previous, relevant experience.

A comprehensive proposal like this can secure work for you, and it can also save you a great deal of wasted effort. Once you are over the initial barrier, your work can be judged on its own merits.

Preparing manuscripts for magazines

These are typed in double spacing with generous margins. The pages should be numbered in sequence and at the bottom of each page there should be an indication that there is more text to follow. This can take several forms – 'more', 'continues', 'mf' (matter follows) are the most common. At the end of the article the word 'ends' should appear.

Some publishers recommend a title page which would include the author's name and address, the title of the article, the length in words, and the date of the manuscript. The title page has two other useful functions. When your article is accepted, the title page is sent to the accounts department as an instruction to pay on publication. However, if your article is rejected, the cover takes the brunt of the punishment in handling. Replace the cover, and you have what is virtually a new manuscript for submission to another publication.

Book manuscripts

Book texts are also typed double-spaced with generous margins. Each chapter should begin on a new page. The numbering of a book manuscript can be either in sequence from beginning to end, or in sequence within chapters. If you are numbering from beginning to end, you must take into account the preliminary material as well as sections such as bibliography and index. Unless the manuscript is typed strictly in sequence this can cause problems, so choose the most practical route.

Publishers ask for two copies of the manuscript; one they retain, and the other is sent to the typesetter. So when you are typing the manuscript you need good carbon paper to make sure that your own copy, the third one, is legible. The alternative is to photocopy.

A book manuscript should be accurate as well as legible. Although an editor or proof-reader will pick up grammatical and spelling mistakes, an author should not rely on them or use them as an excuse for careless work. There are, however, certain situations where the editor may have to change spelling or punctuation, even when it appears to be accurate. Most publishers have their own house rules to cover these points, and they will supply the author with a copy, although they do not do this automatically.

House rules ensure a consistency of spelling and punctuation in the company's books, and act as guidelines for the typesetter, reader, or printer when there is a query. In many cases they are based on *Hart's Rules for Compositors* (Oxford University Press), so an author could use that as a starting point. House rules cover points such as abbreviation, spelling, hyphenation, composite words, numbering, dates, addresses, titles, and the use of capital letters. The house rules of educational or scientific and technical publishers are more stringent to ensure clarity and consistency in their texts.

Scripts

Scripts for radio, television, film and audio visual are more complicated because they include instructions to other people. There are established conventions for laying out scripts, and standard forms of script shorthand to simplify instructions. A script for film, television or audio visual becomes more complex as it advances towards the production stage. The writer is unlikely to be responsible for preparing these detailed instructions, but a practical knowledge of the limitations of production is useful. The books and correspondence courses that deal with script writing cover the technical requirements.

The writer's task in the initial script is to describe the scene, sounds, and characters in a way that can be interpreted by everyone involved in the production process.

Radio scripts have two essential elements, a description of the scene and characters, and the actual sounds to be recorded, dialogue between characters, and sound effects. Dialogue is separated from the rest of the material. The names of all the characters should be listed at the beginning of the script.

Television scripts have several elements — a description of scene, time and place which is the basis of a later shooting script, the dialogue or narative, and the sound effects. Each scene in the script should be numbered, and again the dialogue should be separated from the descriptive material.

The script for a slide-tape presentation is laid out in a more formal structure. The slides are listed on the left-hand side, briefly described, and numbered. On the right-hand side is the commentary that accompanies each slide. When the programme is presented, sound and visual should be synchronised. This basic script layout is sufficient for a programme that uses one or two projectors. When the programme runs on four or more projectors, across several screens, it becomes difficult to describe the results you plan without using a storyboard.

Preparing illustrated material

If illustrations are only a minor part of a book or article, then your task is no more than clearly marking and captioning the photographs or illustrations. But if the project relies equally on text and visual elements, you will need to brief suppliers on the project, and to ensure that what they produce meets the publishers' requirements. In some cases the publishers will want to handle this work themselves, either using staff designers and illustrators or briefing freelance suppliers. In either case you might be consulted or asked to contribute to the briefing.

Briefing photographers, designers and illustrators

You need to provide two different types of information — creative and mechanical. The creative brief describes the task of the illustration or photograph: pictures are not mere decoration. In an illustrated children's book they help to make the text more comprehensible; in a non-fiction book they will be used to clarify a point that cannot be explained by text alone, or to add accurate description where that is important. They should have

101

a specific purpose. To select the right subject the photographer or illustrator will need a copy of your text and an indication of your aims. A sketch of your own ideas, however rough, can usually act as a useful starting point for discussion.

You will also need to supply mechanical detail. This covers the size that the photograph or illustration is to be reproduced in the publication, whether it is to be reproduced in black and white or colour, and the form in which it is to be supplied to the printer. The printer could ask for illustrations as camera-ready artwork or as a transparency or print, so you need to be in close consultation with the printer and the illustrator or photographer.

There are intermediate stages to go through when you are working on an illustrated project. A designer prepares a visual draft for approval before completing artwork or photography. The visual shows the subject matter in very rough form, and also the size and position of the text. Like the writer's synopsis it saves wasted effort and time, and acts as a guide to everyone involved in the project. It is an essential stage in preparing audio-visual programmes, company publications, illustrated books and instructional articles.

Supplying photographs and illustrations

The finished artwork or photographs need to be clearly marked for the publisher. You should supply either a caption or information for someone else to write a caption. The information should include a full description of the subject, with dates where appropriate, and a credit to the supplier or copyright holder.

Each photograph and illustration should be numbered and related to its position in the text. If an illustration has a specific position in the text, in an instruction book for example, you should include a text reference in brackets: (illustration 32) for example. If the photographs or illustrations are grouped together, or used randomly, then you need only identify them and make sure that each has its correct caption.

Captions can be attached to the back of the photograph (by a self-adhesive label) or presented on a separate sheet and numbered. You should supply an additional typed caption sheet which the publisher will mark up for typesetting. If you are borrowing photographs from a collection you will normally be supplied with copy prints. You should tell the owner that these are for reproduction because they need to be good quality.

If you are forced to use an original print for any reason, make sure that the publisher knows, and give instructions not to mark the print in any way. If you don't do that, the print may come back with printers' instructions and scaling marks on it, which could damage the print. The safest procedure is to put the print into a transparent negative bag and write on the bag 'Original. Do not mark.' An alternative is to attach a transparent flap or overlay to the back of the print. This can be used for sizing and instructions.

Handling proofs

All material that is printed goes through a number of production stages after the text has been approved. The writer is a very important part of the proof-reading team even though things seem to be out of his hands.

The first stage is galley proofs, where the text is set in a long continuous strip called a galley. Here the writer is checking for literal errors, omission of material and material in the wrong place; the editor's proof-readers will be looking for the same errors, as well as checking on house style and taking a more critical look at the quality of the typesetting, trying to spot broken characters, incorrect spacing, and considering general appearance.

To mark the proofs the writer should use British Standard proof marks in the margin and in the text. These are found in publications such as *Hart's Rules* and *Writers' and Artists' Year Book*, and they should be made in an obvious colour (usually red, or as requested by the editor). The proof stage is not the time to start changing the text. This should have been done at the editing stage. As a deterrent to people who want to make changes, publishers normally allow a maximum 10 per cent of typesetting costs for author's corrections. Anything over that amount is charged directly to the author.

If first galleys are heavily amended, there may be a second set of galleys to read, but if not, the page make-up should incorporate all the amendments. At the page make-up stage any illustrations will be indicated with their captions. This is the stage to make sure that the right elements belong together. The proofs are marked as before. Some books, however, are set straight to page. This book was set that way.

The final stage of proof-reading is printed proofs, where all the elements are printed on paper. The relationship of text, captions and photos still has to be checked in case of any late slips, but the text should have been settled long before. The problems to look for now are those of quality, to ensure that there are no badly printed or broken characters.

At every stage of proof-reading it is important to turn material around quickly so that the job can progress through its various stages and meet all intermediate target dates. Proof-reading is a skilled profession which the publishers would normally carry out themselves, but authors can act as a double check because of their familiarity with the content. Also, if the authors do not proof-read, any later complaints they have about textual errors may fall on stony ground.

Chapter 12

The Writer's Equipment

A writer needs paper, pencil and a writing surface to start writing. He needs to buy no raw material to make his product, and he does not need an office or a factory to carry out his business.

But to move from this to setting up as a professional writer takes relatively few steps. The professional writer needs to have his material typed for submission to publishers, to keep records of his work programme and his accounts, and to have systems for gathering information. The investment is hardly a major one.

But if the business expands it will incur other costs. These might include photography, reference books, filing cabinets, photocopiers, and other office equipment.

Writing is a low investment business but that should not be an excuse for inefficiency. The professional writer is one who can get hold of his information quickly and get it into publishable form as soon as possible.

Desk and storage

Desks, for example, that incorporate filing drawers are useful. All the records, correspondence and research material can be kept in an easily managed form. There are also desks that incorporate built-in drawing boards. These are useful for people whose work requires a considerable amount of illustration or who design and make up artwork as part of an editorial service. Some people prefer to work directly on to a typewriter, so a desk that is large enough to accommodate one and is also strong enough to take the vibration of the typing is necessary.

Daylight too is desirable, but not always possible: well positioned ceiling lights or desk lamps are a good substitute. Desk lamps should be reasonably heavy or they might bounce around during typing. One of the most useful is the designer's anglepoise lamp which can be adjusted in many different directions to give a direct focused light.

Filing and storage are a problem for any business and writing generates a lot of paper. Ring binders are probably the most common form of storage but eventually they become rather overwhelming. Filing cabinets have a much greater capacity and help you organise your material.

With the development of computer technology, storage becomes more manageable. Texts and correspondence can be held on discs which have a large capacity. Research material is, unfortunately, less manageable because it comes in many different forms.

Storage of research material is likely to remain one of the great paper chases. Magazines and newspaper cuttings, reference books, manuscripts, bibliographies, library catalogues are simply not in a form to be stored on computers. A number of authors have described their methods of storing and retrieving information. Some use the time-honoured method of envelopes or card wallets. Some elaborate it with a card index and others use a comprehensive system of ring binders which are numbered and lettered. Other people just rely on the library system in their area.

Typing and copying

The typewriter is rapidly being overtaken by new technology but the manual portable still has long life ahead of it. Some authors work directly on to a typewriter and then get a final version retyped for submission to a publisher. For the more affluent there are electric typewriters that are quieter, produce better copy and also incorporate correction facilities. Finally, at the top end, are the electronic models that are semi-word processors without the screen and can be linked to a full-scale word processing system.

Carbon paper remains the most economical method of making copies of typed material. The photocopier is useful for taking additional copies, or the one-off copy of research material that you sometimes need. There are small desk-top copiers that are relatively inexpensive but beware of the costs of paper and maintenance which are sometimes built into the contract.

Word processing

A word processor can be a curse or a blessing, depending on

your point of view. This machine is based on a typewriter, but it first displays the text on a screen and stores it on discs. You don't have to print it out until it has been edited and you actually need it on paper. The biggest advantage to the writer is that the text that finally emerges is clean copy. The mistakes are edited out by the author before he prints.

The text can go through as many changes as needed without a total retype. On a full length book of say 50,000 words that could be a substantial task. There may still be a major editing job but the mechanical translation of that into clean copy is minimal.

This is how a word processor works. You type the text on a conventional keyboard. You can also set variables like length of line, character spacing, and inter-line spacing. The text is displayed on a screen: not the whole text, but as much as the screen allows. The screen might show a maximum of 15 lines and the text then moves continuously upwards. The author types until he reaches the end of the text. No need to worry about breaking the text into pages at this stage because the processor handles this automatically when it prints out.

The next stage is to edit the text. You can scroll backwards and forwards through the text and make modifications electronically. It is easy to change characters, amend spelling, put in capitals, embolden characters, underline headings or words, break paragraphs, delete unwanted text, and insert new material wherever it is required. You can also move whole sections of text around as in a cut and paste job. Whole chapters can be rearranged.

When the editing is complete you print out the material. There are a number of printing options available depending on the equipment you have. It can print out with any line spacing you like and it will also number pages for you.

Word processors reduce typewriting problems to a minimum. Provided you can put one or two fingers on a keyboard, you can type clean copy that is easy to read. It cuts down the retyping time and it also prevents loss of manuscript because all the text is stored on a disc, ready for instant replay.

A trend that may grow in the future is sending a disc directly to the publisher or to the typesetter. The disc is then used to provide direct input to a phototypesetting system. Provided the original word processor text is accurate, no new mistakes should occur. New mistakes might happen when a typesetter was keying in new text. As well as ensuring greater accuracy this should also help to reduce costs since one expensive stage of setting is omitted. However, you should remember that the text you submit is unedited. The publisher is likely to have a number of comments, so you may have to wait until text has been edited before submitting a disc.

The only problem is machine compatibility. There is no standard in systems yet and machines do not always take other people's discs. Although special multi-disc readers make type-setting equipment reasonably flexible, few publishers have access to that type of equipment and they could have problems accepting. So if you are thinking of word processing text it pays to check on the compatibility of systems, or send printed copy to your publishers.

ASPIC

The first move to standardise the instructions put on to discs is ASPIC which was published by the British Printing Industries Federation in 1984. ASPIC means Authors Symbolic Prepress Interfacing Codes, and is a method of indicating headings of various levels, paragraph changes, indented text, and other changes to layout. The code is used by the author to indicate his intentions to a designer or typesetter and is not an alternative to either of their skills.

When a publisher reads a disc that is not coded, any instructions to underline or start a new paragraph which might be on the disc can come out as something completely different because of the problems of compatibility between machines. ASPIC helps to remove the possibility of error.

The ASPIC code operates at a number of different levels — essential, standard and special. Essential ASPIC covers different levels of headings, for example chapter head, subhead and secondary subhead, as well as paragraph breaks, indentation of blocks of copy, footnotes, space for diagrams, or language accents. Standard ASPIC indicates other changes including space between lines, changes in type size or type-face and the position of headings. Special ASPIC codes cover the marking of foreign language copy, tabular matter and mathematics.

You put these instructions in at the keyboard as you are typing the text. The ASPIC handbook tells you what the codes are, and you type them within square brackets. Anything that is not enclosed in square brackets is normal text. That means you can type text continuously without making any visible paragraph breaks or separating headings from text. When the disc is read, the codes are translated into machine instructions and the text should emerge as you had planned it. If you want to print out your copy on paper before releasing the disc, you can also put in conventional word processing instructions but you should remove these before releasing the disc.

You need to take a lot of care when you are putting in instructions like this. A machine will only read instructions that are on the disc. If any instructions are omitted the whole exercise could be wasted. The codes that catch people out are the codes at the end of an instruction, for example to stop an indent. If this is omitted the machine will carry on indenting regardless of any other instructions.

The biggest advantage to be gained is a reduction in the typesetting bill. This is certainly an advantage for the publisher, but it is not clear how much time or effort could be saved at the editing stage. If an author's manuscript is revised or amended for punctuation, or changed in content, who would amend the disc, and who then takes responsibility for the accuracy of the disc, and consequently the accuracy of the typesetting? It is quite possible that the cost of corrections to a poor original disc could outweigh any savings the publisher might have by using one.

It is an extra task for the author, so the initiative is more likely to come from the publisher, but 'formatting a disc' may become standard practice as the new technology spreads.

Benefits and costs of word processing

Not all publishers agree that word processing is a benefit. Some feel that it makes the author lazy in his editing. If modifications don't call for a total retype then the writer may not be too fussy about getting the text right. However, it is also true that someone who has the equipment to make changes quickly will make them because it is easy to do so.

Since the first edition of this book, economic word processing has become a reality, due mainly to a series of price innovations by computer manufacturers, Amstrad. At the time of writing it is possible to get a complete word processing package for under £500, including a printer. The company's second breakthrough was to introduce a personal computer that is compatible with the IBM Pesonal Computer for under £1000, with certain models for under £600. You can carry out word processing on the Amstrad or any other personal computer using a variety of different software programs. But, if you use a

109

personal computer rather than a dedicated word processor (one which handles word processing functions only) you can use it for other computing tasks — handling your accounts, getting information from electronic libraries and databanks, filing and sorting information. Gordon Wells' book *Word Processing on a Shoestring* gives a writer's 'consumer guide' to a wide range of low cost systems.

It is also possible to buy electronic typewriters that are just one stage down from word processors. They have the editing functions and a small display screen, and you have the option of typing directly on to paper or previewing on a screen, and printing out multiple or modified versions where the typewriter is hooked up to a compatible printer.

Desktop publishing

Desktop publishing systems take authors one stage beyond word processing and give them a degree of control over the layout and appearance of the text. An author with a desktop publishing system can prepare a 'master' page from which the final document is printed. On the master will be text that is typeset in the correct size, correct typeface and in the correct position. The size and position on the page of the photographs and diagrams is also shown in the master. On more advanced systems, the author can create certain types of diagram — particularly charts, graphs and tables — and can reproduce electronically other existing graphic elements such as photographs, line drawings, logotypes and maps. These facilities and the technical terms are explained in more detail later in this section.

A desktop publishing system will not make you competent in layout and design; it takes considerable training and expertise in the use of the equipment and in the principles of design to achieve that. A desktop publishing system is simply a tool that can be used to achieve results of a certain standard. Whether you can produce masters that are technically and commercially acceptable to a printer or publisher depends on the quality of the results you can achieve and on your relationship with the other party.

Desktop publishing can give the author more control over the finished result when someone else — a printer or publisher for example — is producing the printed version, but it also gives authors who write on specialist topics an opportunity to enjoy economical, low volume publishing which might not have been commercially viable with traditional printing technology.

If your book is being published in normal commercial volumes, the publisher would have built the cost of design and layout into the cost and price of the book. An author's contribution to the process may give some cost savings, but if the results are poor or unacceptable, the savings could be counterproductive – they could lower the quality of the book. Discuss this with your publisher to see whether it would be viable or sensible to provide material for the printer.

If you do wish to proceed, you will probably be asked to provide sample pages so that the quality of the results can be judged. If, however, your proposed book has a specialised market, the offer to supply your own masters for the printer may well sway the publisher's decision. A publishing decision is partially based on an assessment of revenue against costs. A small circulation book will have limited revenue, but if costs can be kept within certain limits, the book could still provide a profitable opportunity for the publisher.

This type of publishing should not be confused with vanity publishing, in which you pay for the whole process of production and distribution. If you decide that the only way to have your specialist work published is to do it yourself, desktop publishing can contribute an important cost saving; the masters for the printer are produced on the desktop publishing system and you have only to add the cost of printing, binding and distribution. An introduction is provided in *Desktop Publishing* by Eric Deeson (Kogan Page). If your work is not up to publication standard, you should not use a desktop publishing system as a way of avoiding a publisher's commercial decision.

However, certain types of publication, suitable for production on a desktop publishing system are likely to become an important part of the market with its own special characteristics. Newsletters are a good example. They give regular reports, reviews and news updates, and can be produced in small quantities and mailed to subscribers. The subscriptions help to cover the cost of production and distribution, and the project could eventually become a profitable one. The *Wordsmith* was an experimental magazine introducing new technology to writers which has subsequently become a regular publication.

We have illustrated three situations in which an author could make effective and economical use of a desktop publishing system. The remainder of this section concentrates on the selection and use of a system. A full description of the characteristics and performance of individual systems is outside the scope of this book, and any information may be out of date because of the rapid changes in the technology of desktop publishing. However, a description in general terms can help you to understand the facilities that various systems are offering. There are three main components to a desktop publishing system — a micro-computer to run the system, software to store instructions, text and typesetting founts, and an output device (printer) to produce the finished piece of paper.

At first sight, a desktop publishing system looks and operates like a word processing system (see pages 106-10), but its functions and performance are much more sophisticated. The software handles all the text entry and editing functions that word processing does, but it also allows you to change the size and style of the type. These are examples of the results you can achieve:

This line is set in 8 point

This line — suitable for a heading — is in 11 point bold

This line, like the rest of this book is in 11 point

The typeface in this line is Baskerville

Here the new line is in Century

The facility to change type style is one of the factors that allows you to give your work its own visual appearance — by varying the style for headings, chapters, tables and emphasis. You can also rearrange units of text and create areas for graphics. A popular way to achieve this is to use a mouse or pointing device. You move the mouse rapidly around the screen to the selected position and work on that area — either putting text there or creating charts and diagrams, using any graphics facilities supplied with the system. When you look at the completed job on the screen, you see it in the form it will be printed — text and diagrams are in the correct position and type is in the right style; this feature is called What You See is What You Get (WYSIWYG).

The completed layout and typesetting are stored on disc until they are needed for printing or updating, in the same way as word processing text is stored. The text is printed on to masters of the correct size for publishing (your printer or publisher can advise you on the correct dimensions) using a special laser printer. This high-speed printer produces good quality results, but for even more professional results — probably beyond the needs of an author — the text can be printed out using a type-setter. These give a greater variety of typefaces and styles; they are designed for commercial use and are naturally expensive.

If you are considering buying a desktop publishing system, you will be faced with a growing choice of equipment — from software packages that can run on existing personal computers like the Amstrad to complete self-contained professional systems. Essentially, you get what you pay for in terms of performance, features and quality of results, but if you can explain your requirements clearly to a dealer you should be able to get a suitable system.

Instructions on how to operate a desktop publishing system come with the equipment — either in the form of a user manual or a demonstration program. Training courses are run by manufacturers, private training organisations and secretarial colleges; they give you the chance to use the equipment under supervision and to gain working experience.

Desktop publishing is an important breakthrough for the author, but it is only a working tool and one that should be used with discretion.

Photography and illustration

If you do your own illustrations a drawing board is essential. There are some good A4 portable models which have the fac-ilities to produce reasonable, squared up artwork. Professional drawing boards with parallel motion are much more expensive, and it would probably be more economical to pay a designer unless illustration was an important part of your offering, and you produced a high volume of work.

It is the same with photography. There are competent amateur or professional photographers who can work to your brief. Sometimes, though, you may want to take your own material, for reference shots or because you happen to be on the spot, for example, at a sports meeting you are already covering.

There is a good range of 35mm SLR automatic cameras which remove much of the guesswork from exposure and focusing, and give you a competent result quite suitable for reproduction in black and white or colour. For colour work, editors are quite happy to work from 35mm transparencies so long as the enlargements are not too great.

Photography manuals give a good guide to the range of films

available. Sports photographers, for example, whether they are shooting in black and white or colour tend to use fast films to cope with the varying light conditions; these may be a bit on the grainy side, but still acceptable. If you are photographing buildings you probably need a finer grain film to capture detail. There is no universal film.

Sound recording

You may find a tape recorder useful, but unless you are collecting material for transmission you don't need to have recording equipment to broadcast standards. In fact, the more portable and unobtrusive the equipment the better. The recorder should be battery operated because there is no guarantee that there will be an accessible mains point. Some people are put off by tape recorders, so the simpler the equipment the better. You can get different types of microphone to achieve particular effects when you are working on location, so it is worth contacting an experienced user for advice.

Some authors use a dictating machine to prepare their text which certainly cuts down the time spent in writing or typing. The only problem is you don't see what you have written until it is typed so there is no chance for early revisions. On the other hand, you know that if it sounds good, it should be easy to read. If you use a dictating machine then you need to contact someone who can do audio typing; otherwise the exercise is wasted. You also need to ensure that your dictation is accurate and clear. Any unusual names or words should be written down.

Videotape recorders

Videotape recorders are useful for recording TV material that you want to study in more detail, particularly for television writers and people who are writing for the educational market. You can record school or Open University programmes if they are broadcast at inconvenient times of the day.

Keeping accounts

You need an efficient method of keeping accounts. A book to record all income and expenditure is adequate if the business is simple, but if you are claiming lots of different expenses then you need a proper accounts book that has columns for analysis.

A calculator is useful if you can't add up and it is also good for working out percentages of expenses claimed when these have to be apportioned between business and personal use.

Keeping the accounts is straightforward with a one-person business but it gets more complicated when the business grows or when several writers are employed.

New technology can help in planning, costing, administration and accounting. The computer is used to record, monitor and update information. Although accounts are less of a problem to the individual writer, they can give the consultancy or the writing business a considerable administrative task.

The recording of chargeable time, for example, can be done on special 'time sheet' software, and any outcosts such as photography, printing or artwork can be collected on 'job bag' software. These are specially developed programs for design studios and advertising agencies but they have equal application in an editorial consultancy. They can also be used to maintain records of work in progress, of project scheduling, and of work completed.

By linking this to an integrated accounting package, the cost and status information can be used for invoicing, cost control, cash flow, and preparing accounts. The financial package could also take care of payroll and other salary/pension functions.

Chapter 13
Business Advice and Finance

Like anyone else running a business, a writer can benefit from professional advice, particularly on financial or legal matters, contracts and authorship, or the problems of running a business. Among the people you are liable to deal with are accountants, bankers, insurance brokers, solicitors and small business consultants, together with specialist advisers on marketing, design, photography and writing.

Banks

Since money is likely to be one of the writer's continuous problems, a friendly bank manager is useful. Individual writers are notorious for their impoverishment; writing income fluctuates wildly and is not something regular that can be relied on to pay the monthly bills. It helps to have a back-up resource when there are long gaps between work and income. Banks can advise on the best methods of financing those gaps and can also be useful in giving advice on the credit rating of customers.

Solicitors

Solicitors can help in several ways depending on the sort of work you handle. If you write books, they can give legal advice on contracts and their implications, or on libel or copyright. If you are handling commercial work, they can advise on terms of business and help to draw up contracts for particular types of project. You may be involved in a team project or partnership; they will help you draw up legal agreements on the requirements of the partnership.

Accountants

When your business gets beyond the basic fee and expenses stage you need the help of an accountant. Individual writers normally have fairly simple accounting requirements because

116

they are not buying and selling material for resale, they may not have business premises to worry about, and they rarely employ staff. But, if business expands and annual turnover exceeds £21,300 (1987-88 figure) they become liable for VAT and must register with HM Customs and Excise. An accountant then becomes very necessary, and can also be a useful source of information on finance as well. Full details of value added tax are given in a handbook available from HM Customs and Excise.

Insurance

You may be legally bound to take out certain types of insurance policy to cover business risks — this would include public liability if you own separate premises; personal sickness insurance and insurance against loss of valuable material such as manuscripts would be advisable for the self-employed writer. Insurance companies can also arrange private pension schemes which are necessary if you are self-employed. It is safest to use a company recommended by the British Insurance Brokers Association, 10 Bevis Marks, London EC3A 7NT; 01-623 9043.

Business consultants

There are also advisers who are specific to your business. The government sponsored or privately run small business advisory services provide guidance on business management. Government agencies such as the Small Firms Service or the Council for Small Industries in Rural Areas (CoSIRA) give a certain amount of free advice initially and then charge for subsequent sessions, while the private ones make a consultancy charge. The offices are listed in telephone directories. There are a number of consultancies based in the universities who specialise in particular types of small business. At the London Business School is the Institute of Small Business Management that advises design groups and advertising agencies. Consultancies like this offer advice on all types of business matters — legal, financial, marketing, administration — but they are probably more useful to a writing company that employs people and is going for particular types of business.

If you plan to specialise in business communications you will find the services of marketing consultants valuable. They research the market, look at the type of service you are offering and identify the most profitable prospects. They can also advise

117

on suitable promotional techniques such as direct mail and other forms of advertising. Marketing consultants are listed in local directories, Yellow Pages or in publications such as *Advertiser's Annual*.

Finance

Chaucer was the first to use the phrase 'the author's empty purse', and to many writers this must seem an appropriate phrase at certain times in their career.

One of the big problems anyone writing for publication faces is the gap between having work commissioned and seeing it in print. With magazines it might be only a month, but with books it could be years. Reducing this gap to a minimum must be the writer's immediate aim but that is not always easy at the beginning of a writing career.

Payment for magazine articles

Magazine articles are paid for at the end of the month of publication. Unfortunately, the month of publication may be some way ahead, particularly if you are entering a new market. The ideal solution is to work for a number of different magazines simultaneoulsy and get a good spread of weekly, monthly and quarterly payments.

Magazine payment is normally at a rate per 1000 words, but there can be enormous variations. Some magazines quote a rate per published page, while others like *Reader's Digest* quote a rate for an entire article. These are published rates; well-known writers with a unique story to sell may be able to do better but, for the majority, the going rate is what they will receive. If you supply your own photographs or illustrations you receive an additional payment for every subject that is published.

Book royalties

Income from books depends on how well your book sells, unless you have accepted an outright fee. Most publishers pay a royalty on sales of the book, but the amount can vary considerably. It is normally around 10 per cent of the published price of each hardback book sold in the UK (equivalent to 15 per cent of the publisher's net receipts), reducing for high-discount sales to wholesalers, multiple retailers and exporters.

However, there are special provisions built into a contract. Trade paperbacks (published by a hardback house) and mass-market paperbacks (published by a paperback house) with their lower cover price and higher volume sales might earn a lower percentage, say 7½ per cent or less.

Royalties are shared when there is more than one contributor to a book, and may be reduced if the publisher contributes a substantial amount of material (illustrations, for example).

There is a whole range of subsidiary rights which give the writer a further percentage on sales or a lump sum. These include a percentage of the net receipts on sales of the UK edition outside this country and at least 50 per cent of the fee paid for a licence to publish the work in specified overseas markets. The sale of translation rights earns a fee which is split between publisher and writer. If your work is sold to a book club you can get a percentage of the fee for rights to publish or of the royalties from sales. You receive a percentage of the fee for anthology, digest and quotation rights and for getting your book serialised in newspapers or magazines: a higher price is paid for serialisation before publication. The right to use some aspect of the book in a commercial context (known as commercial or merchandising rights) can bring in vast sums for successful authors, witness the popularity of Paddington Bear, the illustrations to the *Country Diary of an Edwardian Lady* and Beatrix Potter's characters. When the work is adapted for other media − radio, film, television, video − the author receives a cut. These rights are often reserved by an author or his or her agent as few publishers are geared up to actively selling them If the book is published in a cheaper edition, the author receives a royalty on sales and, in the sad eventuality of the book being remaindered (sold off cheaply to clear stocks), the author gets a percentage of the sum realised after the cost of production has been allowed for.

Advances for books can vary enormously in amount and in the way they are paid. There are no minimum sums or universally accepted methods of calculating them, although there are moves to try to negotiate terms. The total advance paid to the author would not normally exceed the amount the publisher reckons on being earned by the first printing, and is often less. Advances can be made in one lump sum or in parts. A common procedure is to pay in three parts − one on signing the contract, a second on delivery or acceptance of the manuscript, and the third on publication. A good publisher would try to get over half the amount in the writer's hands before publication. The advance is deducted from future royalties for the book. When the royalties exceed the amount of the initial advance, they are usually paid at six-monthly intervals after publication, but some publishers pay annually. You don't always get an advance, particularly with low run special edition books.

There are few circumstances in which publishers or writers should consider outright payment for publication rights. From the publisher's point of view the payment could be too high on a book that sells low. The author might get a high initial payment but lose out on increasing long-term sales or subsidiary rights. However, where the publisher is dealing with a team of writers, the allocation of royalty payments could be very complicated, so it is simpler to pay members of the team a fee that is proportional to their contribution.

Some indication of the way book payments are moving came when the Society of Authors and the Writers' Guild negotiated a new agreement with BBC Publications at the beginning of 1984. The advance for books was set at 55 per cent of royalties from the first printing. There is a sliding scale of royalties which goes from 10 per cent for the first 3000, 12½ per cent on the next 3000, to 15 per cent on sales up to 15,000. A second scale operates on subsequent sales. The publishers also pay up to £150 of the cost of illustrations. Also in the negotiations was an attempt to reduce the period of licensing to 10 years rather than the normal 50-year period of copyright. That is the period in which the BBC is licensed to publish the book. The main aim of the negotiations was to establish the Minimum Terms Agreement with the BBC. The negotiations succeeded in part and the two societies are still trying to implement the agreement with individual publishers.

Fees for radio and television scripts

The Writers' Guild have negotiated a standard minimum fee structure for television scripts which is applied nationally. This fee depends on a number of factors that include the length of the programme, whether it is a network or regional broadcast, and the experience of the writer. The television companies make a distinction between new and established writers. *Writing for the BBC* used to include rates of payment for different types of programme, but this information has not appeared in the latest editions.

BBC and IBA companies differ in the way they make stage payments to script-writers. The BBC pays part on commissioning, part on delivery of the script and part on final acceptance, after any final revisions. IBA companies pay part on commissioning and the rest on delivery. If your idea for a series is accepted, but you do not write all the episodes, you still earn a royalty fee for creating the idea. Radio fees are structured in a similar way, with differentials for new and experienced writers and rates that vary with the length of the broadcast. You can also earn additional fees for talks that you deliver by yourself. The rates for these are quoted in minutes of broadcasting time.

Charging for writing services

If you are providing a writing service, you decide the fee. This would be based on the time you take to do the job multiplied by the hourly rate. You send the client an invoice when the project is completed and, in theory, you should receive payment within 30 days.

That hourly rate should reflect the amount of money it costs to produce the work, the overheads, profits you want to make, and your income requirements. Establishing the rate is not easy because it has to reflect the cost structure and be competitive with the rates of other people. The rate for a job also has to be weighed against its final purpose. If it is a prestige brochure the writing bill is going to be an insignificant part of the total cost. On a simple sales leaflet, writing still plays an important part but a large bill could stand out.

Stage payments are important in writing services, particularly on projects which have a long time span. If the work can be divided into distinct sections, it can be invoiced at the completion of each stage. A convenient breaking point in a brochure would be creative concept, completed text, and delivery of printed brochure. If you are supervising other aspects of the project for your client — design, photography, or print, for example — you need to negotiate stage payments, so that you have the funds available to pay the suppliers.

Grants and awards

Direct fees are not the only source of income for a writer. Grants, awards and prizes can make a useful supplement. Over 100 annual prizes are available for books, poetry, broadcasting or essays. The National Book League publish the *Guide to Literary Prizes, Grants and Awards*, and the magazine *The Author* publishes details of new awards as they are announced.

Literary prizes cover many different categories. The Nobel Prize for Literature awarded to an author for a body of literature, and the Booker McConnell Prize, awarded for a specific title, are perhaps the most famous but the variety is enormous — the W H Smith & Son Annual Literary Award, H E Bates Short Story Competition, Sid Chaplin Literary Award for writing about new towns, Children's Book of the Year Award, Thomas Cook Travel Book Award, Gold Dagger Award for non-fiction crime, Wolfson Literary Awards for History or The Times Educational Supplement Information Book Awards.

These are national awards, but there is also a thriving regional and local award system — Wandsworth All London Literary Competition, Scottish Arts Council Awards and awards from the other regional arts councils. Many local competitions offer prizes for short stories, essays or poems, often on local themes. These local competitions are announced in the regional arts magazines and you can find details circulated in public libraries.

You would submit your own entry to a local or regional competition, but the submissions for national awards are usually made by publishers. Some competitions only accept work that is previously unpublished, and then demand the right to publish winning entries. For a professional writer the loss of royalty income and other rights could outweigh the immediate advantages of the prize or award, so study the conditions carefully.

Grants are given to complete work in progress. The Arts Council make a number of grants for different types of work. Their grants to writers are given to people who have already had work published and have another project commissioned. The grants are for a specific period of time and the writers are nominated by publishers or other sponsors. Each of the regional arts councils gives grants to encourage local writing and there are a number of private schemes.

The Arts Council also make grants to publishers, either to subsidise an unprofitable work of creative writing or to contribute to the publishing costs of literary magazines of a high standard. Their grants help to keep poetry in print.

Public Lending Right

Since 1983 writers have had a new source of income in Public

Lending Right (PLR) — a payment on books that are borrowed from public libraries. In the year ended January 1987, almost 13,000 authors received payments totalling some £2.4 million on 113,500 registered books.

There was a strong campaign to introduce PLR, and one of its main arguments was the high level of lost income that library borrowing represented. True, the author received royalties on the books that were sold to the libraries, but he received nothing for subsequent borrowing. If a borrower takes four books each week, that represents potential book sales of £10 to £20 per week. With 11,000 libraries in the country there were an awful lot of sales getting away.

PLR is intended to reflect the level of borrowing throughout the country and to give authors an income based on that. It would be extremely difficult and expensive to monitor borrowings from all 11,000 libraries so a sample is used and the number of borrowings multiplied to give a national figure. There are 16 libraries around the country in the sample, of which four change every year.

Not all the registered authors earned money because the bottom limit for payment is £1. Each loan earned the author 1.20p and the annual earnings ranged from £1 up to the maximum £5000. Some of the higher earners decided not to claim their PLR. They realised that virtually all of it would go back to the Inland Revenue, so they left it in the pool for others.

To qualify for PLR you have to be an eligible author with an eligible book, even if you are not the copyright owner. An eligible author is resident in the UK and has his name on the title page of the book. There can be up to three joint authors of a book, but under current legislation, if one of them dies, the book ceases to qualify. An eligible book must be printed and bound and have a minimum number of pages — 32 if it is prose or illustration, and 24 if it is poetry or drama. You can register any number of eligible books in the scheme, and, if one of your books is published in volumes, each volume counts as a separate entry.

You can get application forms from the Registrar of PLR, PLR Office, Bayheath House, Prince Regent Street, Stockton-on-Tees TS18 1DF, and you should return these by 30 June of the preceding year to receive payment in the following February. The application form also asks for information about you and the books, and it stresses the need to include an ISBN (International Standard Book Number) for each book. The

ISBN is a critical number. Libraries use it to keep track of the borrowings on their computer and it is the code that is used to allocate earnings to a particular book.

Public Lending Right could prove to be a significant gain for authors in the long term. With the high price of books and the squeeze on publishers' profit margins, many people look to libraries' stock as their main source of books, and will do so all the more should VAT be imposed on them.

Business costs

Writing is a low-cost business but you still need to record your costs carefully — either to charge them to a customer or to claim some of them as allowable expenditure against income tax.

If you are preparing manuscripts for publication or broadcasting you would not charge the publisher or producer for your costs; you would receive a fee for the work you produce. However, where you are writing to a commercial brief you would make a charge which is based on a combination of overheads and direct costs.

Overheads are costs that you incur continuously; they are the costs of running the business and might include rent or mortgage, rates, telephone, stationery, secretarial assistance, business equipment, car running costs. Direct costs are only incurred on a specific job and might include photographer's fees, research documents, special travelling — to a customer's research laboratory, for example — and any materials related to the job.

When you charge a customer for a job you include all the direct costs and a proportion of the overheads. If it costs you £40 per week to meet overheads, and you work 40 hours per week, your hourly overhead rate is £1. The hourly rate charged to the customer would also include the amount you pay yourself plus any profit you wish to make. So a chargeable rate of £10 per hour might be made up of £1 overheads, £7 salary, £2 profit. The difference between the amount you charge the customer and your costs is the operating profit, and your aim should be to make that as large as possible.

If you are earning a fixed fee from published or broadcast material, you can still look at your work from the point of view of profitability. Although you cannot increase the amount you earn you may decide that certain types of work are not profitable. If you calculate that it costs £10 an hour to run the business, including overheads, salary and profit, then a £150 article that takes eight hours is clearly more profitable than a £25 article that takes four. A £1000 commercial writing job that takes over 60 hours is also less profitable than the £150 article, but few writers would want to refuse that kind of sum, so profitability is not the only criterion. You might, for example, want to establish yourself in a particular market, so it would be worth while writing for less to get your name in the right publications.

Costs and income tax

The amount of income tax you pay is also based on your profits, but these profits are not operating profits — they are the difference between your income from writing and your allowable business expenditure. To calculate this and to meet the requirements of the Inland Revenue you need to keep a set of accounts, or employ an accountant to do that for you.

The accounts of an individual writer should be straight-forward. Writers don't hold stocks, make cash sales, employ large numbers of people, own machinery or factories, or make capital investment programmes. The expenditure side of the business is simple but you still need to keep accurate records.

If you work from home you can claim part of the running costs of your home — 25 per cent would be a reasonable proportion. You should include gas and electricity bills together with a proportion of telephone rental. If you have your own business premises then you would claim all the costs — rent, rates, heating, lighting, telephone and maintenance — because the building is being used exclusively for your business.

You can claim all the costs of running the business — stationery, pens, pencils, drawing equipment, postage, charges for telephone calls, photographic costs, subscriptions to professional bodies, the costs of any suppliers you use such as printers, designers, accountants or illustrators. Travelling costs can only be claimed if they are exclusively for business. So if you took a train to London to see your publisher, that is allowable; if you drove to a reference library or to visit a client, that is allowable; but if you drive to your own office that is not allowable. When you use a car in the business you need to record your total mileage and your genuine business mileage. What you can then claim is a percentage of all the car running costs including petrol, road tax, insurance and maintenance.

Research material is an allowable expenditure for a writer. It includes the costs of reference books, magazines, newspapers and possibly television rental. Those expenses come under the heading of current expenditure: that is they are used up in the course of an accounting year.

If you employ anyone in the business on a full- or part-time basis you would claim the cost of that employee's salary as an allowable expense. If you employ a number of people in a company, the procedures become much more complicated, and lie outside the scope of this book.

Whatever form of expenditure you claim, you should be able to substantiate it by keeping records, and also by retaining receipts. One simple way of recording income is to give every payment you receive a number and to write out an invoice, where you record the details of the writing service, article or book, even if you do not normally invoice a publisher.

Your accounts should cover a period of 12 months. Your accounting year does not have to coincide with the income tax year. It could commence on 1 January and finish on 31 December. At the end of that year, your accounts should show all the income you received, minus all your allowable current business expenditure. That is your profit. You then subtract any capital allowances you are claiming to give your taxable profit. To determine how much tax you actually pay, you also have to deduct personal tax allowances such as married man's allowance, or personal pension contributions.

Income tax is normally assessed on what is called a preceding year basis; you are assessed on the profits of your accounting year that ended in the previous tax year. If your accounting year ended each year on 5 January, for the 1987-88 tax year you would be assessed on the profits you made in the 1986-87 tax year — that is, the profits in your accounts ending on 5 January 1987. If your business is just starting the rules for first year tax assessment are more complicated. You can get advice on this from your accountant, the Inspector of Taxes, or a guide such as *Which Tax Saving Guide* or any of the series of small business books published by Kogan Page, listed on page 136.

As well as income tax you, as a self-employed person, are also liable to pay Class 4 National Insurance contributions. These are based on your profits, and you are liable to pay them if your profits exceed certain limits. You can get information on the current limits from the tax office or from the Department of Health and Social Security.

Chapter 14

Running a Writing Business

Writing is essentially a profession for the individual. You stand or fall by your own ability and efforts, but it is interesting to see how other writers have fared. One of the most prolific authors was Arnold Bennett who wrote at least one novel every year and was a regular contributor to newspapers and magazines. His annual output in numbers of words was quite phenomenal and he was accused by many of being a business-man before being a writer.

Bennett's prodigious output in so many different fields was unmatched by any author, but in the 1980s Keith Waterhouse is showing similar versatility. In a television profile he acknowl-edged a debt to Bennett. Waterhouse's weekly stint includes a column for the *Daily Mirror* and a piece for *Punch*; he has written or collaborated on television plays and has written novels. Like Bennett he does not believe that the writer should be tied to any one medium and he feels sure that Arnold Bennett would have been in television if he had lived to see it.

Anthony Burgess in his early career covered a fair amount of ground. Although he is best known for writing novels, he wrote the film script for *A Clockwork Orange*, was drama critic for the *Spectator*, wrote stage plays and later tackled literary translations, including a project to translate *Ulysses* into Italian. But Burgess's real potential was shown when he produced five novels in one year. He had been told by his doctors that he had a brain tumour, and that he had only a short time to live — about a year in fact. He poured all his energy into his novels.

His publisher worried about this but Burgess went ahead and succeeded. Unfortunately, it backfired a couple of years later when he received the royalties for all this work. Burgess suddenly became embarrasingly rich and had to leave the country because of the very high tax bills he was faced with.

A different situation faced Simon Raven when he was commissioned by a publisher to produce a book. Raven knew that the project was likely to take a long time so he was paid a salary by the publisher while he worked on the manuscript over a period of five years. The publisher's faith was commendable, but was fully justified when he produced the book which turned out to be a best-seller — the first of many in the series *Alms for Oblivion*.

For sheer volume of output it must be hard to rival Barbara Cartland. According to television profiles she sets herself a daily total which she adheres to strictly. Like a number of prolific writers she makes the most of good secretarial assistance to complement her own writing talent.

John Braine adequately expressed the frustration of the part-time novelist; he was trying to do a job that he hated during the day, and then picking up the novel again in the evening. He talked about the problems of frequent rejection of his first novel and the agony of having a play that was a financial and critical failure. During the day Braine was working as a librarian, a situation he described as being like a eunuch in a harem The job was not physically demanding, it simply drained him of all his energy. When he succeeded with the novel *Room at the Top*, the immediate failure receded but the possibility was always hovering.

But if the problem is rejection then what about the possibility of actually publishing yourself, not as a last resort but as part of your life. Some might argue that this would lead to a trail of lower quality material, but take a look at just two people who could hardly be called second-rate writers — Virginia Woolf and Althea Braithwaite. Virginia Woolf and her husband Leonard owned the Hogarth Press, who published all her books and gained a fine reputation as publishers of quality literature. Althea Braithwaite is best known to children as the Althea of the Dinosaur Press at Cambridge. They specialise in illustrated children's books and Althea writes many of them herself. The books are highly regarded and are an accepted part of the school curriculum. In neither case has the quality of the writing or publishing suffered.

Another writer/publisher is Clive Birch who is managing editor of Barracuda Books, a company he set up in 1974. Barracuda specialise in limited edition, high quality books for special interest groups. Much of his output has been books on local history which have a primarily local market. Few of these have a print run over 1000 and all are sold by the subscription method which has succeeded in 95 per cent of the cases.

But Clive Birch also writes books himself — several local history books, and a book on the Corporation of London. He enjoys writing, but as a publisher he finds there is a distinct advantage in being in touch with the writer's problems. In some cases the help he can give is very direct — like the advice to the author who produced 135,000 words for a book of 25,000, or the occasion when he had to sit coaxing an author who had lost his nerve a few weeks before the manuscript was due to be delivered.

Team writing

Although writers spend most of their career working alone, there may be occasions when cooperation with other writers, or other professionals, can be an advantage. Team writing is increasingly common in educational publishing and in the production of illustrated non-fiction books or partworks. In television, writers, producers and actors often combine to put forward a proposal for a new programme or series, and in business communications large-scale projects may be beyond the capacity of the individual.

Team writing has its complications, though. The first problem is to get the mix of the team right. You are relying on the skills and attitudes of other people. They have to be able to work together and to produce the results. From the outset you need to establish who has responsibility for different elements of the project, and who makes the final decision on whether team members' contributions are acceptable. If there is a formal team leader that person has to set targets for progress and to make sure that all the members make their proper contributions. There should not be an unnecessary load on one member.

A team can have a formal or informal relationship. A publisher might take the initiative and bring a team together to work on just one project, or the initiative may come from the team itself. This also helps to determine the way the team shares fees or royalties. A simple method would be to divide project income on a proportional basis that relates to the contribution made by each member. Where the income is a single fee, for providing business writing services, for example, the calculations are straightforward.

Books are more difficult. Royalty income is likely to spread over a number of years and an informal team is unlikely to stay together for any length of time. An alternative would be to pay a single fee to team members who make a small contribution and to confine shared royalties to the major contributors. The same problem applies to acknowledgements. Each member of the team should be acknowledged for his or her contribution, but it may not be practical or profitable to name them all as co-authors. Too many authors on the title page could make a book ineligible for Public Lending Right — the maximum is three.

Partnerships

A partnership is a more formal arrangement between two or more people who find they are working together regularly. The members may not necessarily be working as a team on the same project, but may be carrying out similar types of work and find it beneficial to share premises or resources, or to complement each other's skills.

If you are entering a formal partnership, you should carefully consider the legal implications. As a partner you are equally responsible with the other members for the debts of your organisation. In one sense, this is better than your position as a self-employed individual, where you have sole responsibility for your debts, but you must have trust and confidence in your partners. Any such arrangement should be the subject of a legal agreement.

Employing other writers

As an individual or a partner, you may wish to expand your activities by employing other writers on a permanent basis. To the writing and running of your business, you would add the administrative tasks of an employer. You are responsible for collecting the employee's income tax and National Insurance contributions. You must take out employer's compulsory liability insurance, and comply with the Health and Safety at Work Act. With employment law becoming increasingly complex, you need to be fully aware of your own and your employees' rights and obligations. You can get more information on tax and National Insurance from the tax office or from the DHSS.

If you plan to employ other writers the first task is to make sure that you recruit the right people. If you have specific tasks for the employee, you are looking for a particular type of writer, but you are more likely to be looking for someone who is versatile enough to tackle a wide variety of tasks. You need to find out about the writer's experience and to see examples of previous work. When you employ people you have to keep them busy to remain profitable, so you have to be certain of a continuous workload.

Chapter 15
Further Information

Since much of what you write will be helping other people to learn, it follows that you should spend a lot of time reading, to keep up to date with progress in your own field, and to learn from other writers. On pages 134-6 is a bibliography of material that is useful to the writer, as well as addresses of organisations that you may wish to contact. Some of this information is discussed in more detail below.

Books on writing techniques

There is a growing literature on the techniques of writing. Although they have always been available, the number of books was limited and they tended to concentrate on writing fiction or technical reports. Now there is a series of specific textbooks on techniques for different media in the 'How to Write' series. These books grew out of the work of the Arvon Foundation for writing studies. Their books cover novels, children's books, television, poetry and writing generally. They are all written from the point of view of the person who is new to writing, stimulating enthusiasm and covering basic techniques. Although they are aimed primarily at beginners, the sections on technique are sound, and would be useful to a writer who is moving into a new medium.

There are 'how to' books on TV, radio, film and audio-visual media as well. The BBC produces a guide to market opportunities, *Writing for the BBC*, which gives full details of the organisation of the company and the way it operates. For film writers there is *The Writer and the Screen* which adequately explains the concept of screenplay. There are also published transcripts of plays and filmscripts.

Ken Russell's book *An Appalling Talent* gives a good insight into the way a screenplay changes when it gets into the hands of a director. It describes how he copes with many ideas at once, and how he actually gets any of these into production.

A number of other books cover similar ground. Dianne

Doubtfire's *Craft of Novel Writing* and *Teach Yourself Creative Writing* give good advice on technique and discuss the problems of contracts. Gordon Wells produced a very good guide for the non-fiction writer called *The Successful Author's Handbook*. This deals primarily with the production of textbooks for the non-fiction, technical and educational markets, and it clearly explains the techniques of turning initial concepts into a sales presentation for the publisher. He followed this up with *Craft of Writing Articles* which deals specifically with material for magazines. This is more of a how-to-do-it book for the non-writer. His previous book was aimed at the professional writer moving into books, or the subject expert who has to go into print.

John Braine's excellent book *Writing a Novel* is a very good guide to the creative process in action. Literary biographies or autobiographies like Virginia Woolf's *A Writer's Diary* give the same sort of insight. The *Paris Review* interviews collected under the title *Writers at Work* show the variety of attitudes and working methods that writers adopt.

The publisher's view

The publisher's point of view is important to the author. Two excellent books by Michael Legat — *Dear Author* and *An Author's Guide to Publishing* — cover this ground admirably, and point out many of the problems that people in publishing have to solve. He indicates common faults that authors should avoid, and that publishers have to deal with. He also discusses most of the misconceptions people have about publishing and the way their work is handled.

Magazines on writing

To keep up to date with opportunities and developments it is important to read magazines on writing and related topics. *The Author* and *Contributor's Journal* are perhaps the most relevant but there is a great deal of useful information in *Campaign*, the *Listener*, *Stage and Television Today*, the *Bookseller*, *Freelance Writing & Photography*, and the *Arts Guardian*.

Courses for writers

At many American universities there are schools of journalism and creative writing. Britain has nothing similar although the NUJ/NPA runs a joint training scheme for journalists only. A number of correspondence schools such as the Writing School offer writing courses, and these are very useful for learning about markets and the mechanical requirements of different media. They may be useful for learning about new media. The Arvon Foundation was one of the first organisations to try to fill the gap in writing education. They run residential courses for writers, where the writer works closely with a tutor who is himself a successful full-time writer. There are also a number of part-time courses run around the country.

Bibliography

General guides to writing opportunities

The titles marked with an asterisk may not be in print or difficult to get, but most should be available through the public library service.

Benn's Media Directory (Benn Publications Ltd) annual
British Rate and Data (Maclean-Hunter) monthly
Getting Published, George Kay (New Horizons)
Successful Author's Handbook, Gordon Wells (Macmillan)
Teach Yourself Creative Writing, Dianne Doubtfire (Hodder and Stoughton)
The Way to Write, John Fairfax and John Moat (Elm Tree Books)
Willing's Press Guide (Thomas Skinner Directories) annual
Writers' and Artists' Year Book (A & C Black) annual

Techniques for books and magazines

Craft of Novel Writing, Dianne Doubtfire (Allison & Busby)
Craft of Writing Articles, Gordon Wells (Allison & Busby)
How to Write Articles that Sell, Perry Wilbur (Wiley)
Magazine Article Writing,* Mary T Dillon (The Writer Inc)
Non-fiction,* David St John Thomas (David & Charles)
The Way to Write for Children, Joan Aiken (Elm Tree Books)
Writing a Novel, John Braine (Eyre Methuen)
Writing Fiction, R V Cassill (Prentice-Hall)

Writing for radio, theatre and screen

Playmaking,* William Archer (Chapman & Hall)

Radio Drama, Ian Rodger (Macmillan)
Radio Plays,* Giles Cooper (BBC Publications)
Scriptwriting for Television,* Janet Dunbar (Museum Press)
Techniques of Radio Journalism,* John Herbert (A & C Black)
The Way to Write for Television, Eric Paice (Elm Tree Books)
The Writer and the Screen,* Wolf Rilla (W H Allen; out of print)
Writing for the BBC (BBC Publications)
Writing for Television,* Malcolm Hulke (A & C Black)
Writing for Television Today,* Arthur Swinson (A & C Black)

Mechanics of writing

Camera Journalism,* A E Woolley (A S Barnes & Co)
Daily Mirror Style, Keith Waterhouse (Mirror Books)
Indexes and Indexing,* Robert L Collison (Ernest Benn)
Newsman's English, Harold Evans (Heinemann)
Research, Ann Hoffmann (A & C Black)

Biographical material

Authors by Profession, Victor Bonham-Carter (Society of
    Authors)
The Making of a Novelist, Margaret Thomson-Davis (Allison
    & Busby)
The Modern Short Story,* H E Bates (Michael Joseph)
The Novel Today, ed Malcolm Bradbury (Fontana)
Novelists on the Novel, Miriam Allott (Routledge & Kegan Paul)
The Working Novelist,* V S Pritchett (Chatto & Windus)
Writers at Work, The *Paris Review* Interviews (Secker &
    Warburg)
A Writer's Diary, Virginia Woolf (Hogarth Press)
A Writer's Notebook, Somerset Maugham (Heinemann)

The publisher's viewpoint

An Author's Guide to Publishing, Michael Legat (Hale)
Dear Author,* Michael Legat (Pelham Books)
*Publishing and Bookselling: A History from the Earliest Times to
    the Present Day*, F A Mumby and Ian Norris (Bell & Hyman)
The Publishing Game, Anthony Blond (Jonathan Cape)
Reader's Report,* Christopher Derrick (Gollancz)
The Truth about Publishing, Sir Stanley Unwin (George Allen
    & Unwin)

Magazines and newspapers about writing

Arts Council regional reviews
Audio Visual, PO Box 109, Maclaren House, Scarbrook Road, Croydon CR9 1QH
The Author (Society of Authors)
The Bookseller, 12 Dyott Street, London WC1A 1DF
Campaign, 22 Lancaster Gate, London W2 3LY
Contacts, 42 Cranbourn Street, London WC2
Contributor's Bulletin, Freelance Press Services, 5-9 Bexley Square, Salford, Manchester M3 6DB
Creative Review, 60 Kingly Street, London W14 5LH
Freelance Writing & Photography (see *Contributor's Bulletin* above)
Guardian (from newsagents)
The Listener (from newsagents)
Production and Casting Report, Jaguar Books, 280 Lordship Lane, London SE22
Radio Times (from newsagents)
Spotlight (see *Contacts* above)
The Stage and Television Today, 47 Bermondsey Street, London SE1 3XT
The Times Literary Supplement (from newsagents)
TV Times (from newsagents)
Writers' Monthly, The Writer Ltd, PO Box 34, St Andrews KY16 9RH

Business reading

Financial Management for the Small Business, Colin Barrow (Kogan Page)
Law for the Small Business, Patricia Clayton, 5th edition (Kogan Page)
The Word Processing Handbook, John Derrick and Phillip Oppenheim (Kogan Page)
Working for Yourself: The Daily Telegraph Guide, Godfrey Golzen (Kogan Page)

Professional advice

For specialised advice on writing, the Writers' Guild and the Society of Authors are the most influential groups. The Writers' Guild have particular interests in screen and television, and have negotiated regularly with the broadcasting authorities. The

Society of Authors have stronger interests in book authorship but the two have successfully cooperated on a number of occasions, notably in their efforts to establish the Minimum Terms Agreement with publishers and in the introduction of Public Lending Right.

The Society of Authors
The Society of Authors (address on page 139) provide information about agents and publishers, and advise on negotiations and contracts with these parties. They take up complaints on their members' behalf and will take legal action if they feel that a problem could have detrimental effects on writers generally.

The Society has a number of special groups within the general organisation – Translators Association, Broadcasting Group, Educational Writers Group, Children's Writers Group, Technical Writers Group and Medical Writers Group. These groups are looking closely at developments within their own fields and publish a number of leaflets and handbooks on their work.

Members of the Society receive a regular copy of *The Author* and can get free copies of leaflets on subjects such as income tax, National Insurance, and copyright. The Society also offers useful benefits to the self-employed such as group membership of the Retirement Benefit Scheme, BUPA, Pension Fund and the Contingency Fund.

You can join the Society as a full or an associate member. To qualify as a full member you need to have a full-length work published or an established reputation in another medium. Associate members should have a full-length work accepted for publication, or shorter work already published.

The Writers' Guild
The Writers' Guild (address on page 139) represent the interests of people who are primarily writing for stage, film or television. Their negotiations with broadcasting authorities have resulted in improved payments for everyone writing in these media, and they are working towards standard terms and minimum agreements. They have a standard agreement with the BBC for radio writers and national agreements with the television companies covering minimum fees, going rates, copyright licence, credits, terms and conditions.

Like the Society of Authors, they are studying developments within the industry, for example looking at the implications of video cassettes and video disc.

The Guild is affiliated to the TUC and regards itself as the writers' trade union. Though its origins are in film and television it now has interests in all areas of publishing and broadcasting. To qualify for full membership of the Guild you need to have a full-length book published, a feature film released, or an hour-long television or radio play broadcast. If you have had shorter work produced, that helps you to accumulate points for full membership. If you are writing for any of these media you can qualify for associate membership.

Other groups

The Society and the Guild are the main groups but for writers with particular interests there are a number of other societies. If you are in business communications the Institute of Practitioners in Advertising, the Institute of Public Relations, the British Association of Industrial Editors, and the Institute of Scientific and Technical Communicators are relevant to your activities. The British Film Institute, the Association of Independent Producers and the Theatre Writers' Union cater for people writing for film and theatre.

The National Union of Journalists (address on page 139) is the main group representing people who write for the press; like the Institute of Journalists they maintain a register of freelance specialist writers which is circulated free to publishers to get work for members.

Professional associations

Arts Council of Great Britain, 105 Piccadilly, London W1V 0AU; 01-629 9495

The Association of Authors' Agents, Secretary, 20 John Street, London WC1N 2DL

The Association of Illustrators, 1 Colville Place, London W1P 1HN; 01-636 4100

Book Trust (previously known as the National Book League), Book House, 45 East Hill, Wandsworth, London SW18 2QZ; 01-870 9055

British Film Institute, 127 Charing Cross Road, London WC2H 0EA; 01-437 4355

British Institute of Professional Photography, Amwell End, Ware, Hertfordshire SG12 9HN; 0920 4011

Crime Writers' Association, PO Box 172, Tring, Hertfordshire HP23 5LP; 01-353 2644

The Institute of Journalists, Bedford Chambers, Covent Garden, London WC2E 8HA; 01-836 6541

The Institute of Scientific and Technical Communicators Ltd, 17 Bluebridge Avenue, Brookmans Park, Hatfield, Hertfordshire AL9 7RY; (Potters Bar) 0707 55392

National Union of Journalists, Acorn House, 314 Gray's Inn Road, London WC1X 8DP; 01-278 7916

The Poetry Society, 21 Earls Court Square, London SW5 9DE; 01-373 7861

Publishers Association, 19 Bedford Square, London WC1B 3HJ; 01-580 6321

The Society of Authors, 84 Drayton Gardens, London SW10 9SD; 01-373 6642

The Society of Indexers, Secretary Mrs H C Troughton, 16 Green Road, Birchington, Kent CT7 9JZ; 0843 41115

The Writers' Guild of Great Britain, 430 Edgware Road, London W2 1EH; 01-723 8074

Useful addresses

Alliance of Small Firms and Self-Employed People, 42 Vine Road, East Molesey, Surrey KT8 9LF; 01-979 2293

Arvon Foundation, Lumb Bank, Hebden Bridge, West Yorkshire HX7 6DS

Association of Conference Executives Ltd, 72 Ermine Street, Huntingdon, Cambridgeshire PE18 6EZ; 0480 57595

BBC (Radio), Broadcasting House, London W1A 1AA; 01-580 4468

BBC External Services, Bush House, Strand, London WC2B 4PH; 01-240 3456

BBC (Television), Television Centre, Wood Lane, London W12 7RJ; 01-743 8000

British Association of Picture Libraries and Agencies, PO Box 284, London W11 4RP

Council for Small Industries in Rural Areas (CoSIRA), 141 Castle Street, Salisbury, Wiltshire SP1 3TP; 0722 336255

Council for Subject Teaching Association, c/o Mr A R Hall, 117 Valley View Road, Rochester, Kent ME1 3NX

Guild Sound and Vision Ltd, Woodston House, Oundle Road, Peterborough PE2 9PZ; 0733 315315

HM Customs and Excise, VAT Administration Directorate, King's Beam House, Mark Lane, London EC3R 7HE; 01-626 1515. Contact your local office.

Inland Revenue, Contact your local Inspector of Taxes.

Independent Broadcasting Authority, 70 Brompton Road, London SW3 1EY; 01-584 7011

National Federation of Self-employed and Small Businesses Ltd, 32 St Anne's Road West, Lytham St Annes, Lancashire FY8 1NY; 0253 720911

140 Lower Marsh, London SE1 7AE; 01-928 9272

School Government Publishing Company, Darby House, Bletchingley Road, Merstham, Redhill, Surrey RH1 3DN; (Merstham) 07374 2223

School Library Association, Liden Library, Barrington Close, Liden, Swindon SN3 6HF; 0793 617838

Small Firms Service, Department of Employment. Contact regional offices by telephoning the operator on 100 and asking for Freefone Enterprise.

The Writing School, 18-20 High Road, London N22 6BR; 01-888 1242

Index